INDIAN
FOOD
MADE EASY

Anjum Anand

INDIAN FOOD MADE EASY

Anjum Anand

Photographs by Vanessa Courtier

METRO BOOKS
NEW YORK

This 2008 edition published by Metro
Books, by arrangement with Quadrille
Publishing Limited

Editorial director Anne Furniss
Creative director Helen Lewis
Project editor Gillian Haslam
US editor Eleanor Van Zandt
Designer Lucy Gowans
Photographer Vanessa Courtier
Food styling Susie Theodorou
Props styling Wei Tang
Production Vincent Smith, Ruth Deary

Metro Books
122 Fifth Avenue
New York, NY 10011

ISBN-13: 978-1-4351-0780-9
ISBN-10: 1-4351-0780-2

Printed and bound in China
10 9 8 7 6 5 4 3 2 1

To my dearest
daughter, whose
second full
sentence was
"Mama, what you
cooking?" The
answer, my
darling,
was this.

Contents

Introduction

The unknown can be daunting. I suppose this is why in Britain, where I now live, relatively few people ever cook Indian food—despite the enormous popularity of Indian restaurants.

But as with many challenges in life, once you climb that hill and face those fears, they were never as tough as you imagined and the rewards can be . . . well, delicious. At least they are in the case of Indian food! And with the fantastic supply of ingredients now available in many supermarkets or at the touch of a button on the Internet, there are no more excuses for not cooking something you love to eat. Indian cuisine seems to be surrounded by an aura of mystery and myths, but the truth is anyone can cook it. And that is the aim of this book—to show you just how quick and simple the recipes can be.

Indian cuisine has always been very straightforward—you cooked what grew locally, and along with a helping of bread or rice, that was it. It was and still is a regional and seasonal food, which has had spices woven into its very DNA, as they are considered the elixir of health. It is, at heart, peasant food, eaten as much for taste as it is for nourishment. Meals traditionally consisted of some protein, a vegetable, and a staple. The number of dishes served at any one meal did increase with prosperity, which, as many lived in joint families with lots of people there to help in the kitchen, was fine.

However, things have changed, and people now have less time to devote to culinary tasks. Indian food has always been an integral part of my diet, and long ago I felt the need to simplify, streamline, and lighten my meals. I really wanted to bring this fantastic, complex, and generous cuisine into the twenty-first century. Food is personal—you cook what you want to eat—so cooking an Indian meal can be as easy as baking some fish, broiling some chicken, stir-frying spinach, or rustling up some rice and lentils.

The accepted "wisdom" that Indian food is unhealthful is an unfair allegation. Indian restaurants are not representative of how Indians eat; we don't add cream, ghee, or nut pastes to all of our dishes. This cuisine can seem oily, but so can the Mediterranean diet, and I think oil is good, when consumed in moderation. And since the cooked accompaniments that required oil were traditionally served in small portions, with either boiled rice or simple bread, you would have needed the oil to stay healthy. Most Indians eat well-balanced, nutritious meals incorporating vegetables, lentils, whole grains, dairy, and a little meat or fish—all fresh food and fantastic ingredients. What we see as Indian food is often a murky narration of the truth with much lost in translation. The food is, actually, inherently very healthful.

In Britain, Indian food has been on a journey of evolution. We have moved on from inauthentic creamy, fruity curries and can now easily find tandoori and regional options. But there is still so much to discover. India is a country that has so much to offer. It is food that is eaten for breakfast, lunch, and dinner. It is everyday food; food for children, adults, friends, and family. But every cuisine has all these elements, so why has the obvious escaped us for so long? Why has Indian food been relegated to the upper shelves of bookstores—the back bench of the United Nations of Cookery and out of most people's reach for so long?

It has been a long road getting here and a slow but exciting journey, but thankfully we can now experience Indian food the way it was intended, at home.

The Indian Kitchen Made Easy

You can make Indian food without having to buy any new cooking equipment, but if you like cooking Indian food, or in fact any ethnic meal, there are a few items that make the experience easier.

Nonstick karahi

No self-respecting healthy eater would be without nonstick cookware. A karahi is a woklike pan with a rounded base. The curved bottom allows the food to move easily in the pan without bits of food sticking to and burning in the edge. Once you start to use these pans, you'll never want to go back to straight-sided saucepans.

Curved cast-iron pan (tava)

We cook most of our flat breads on this shallow, concave cast-iron pan. The pan holds the heat well, and the bread cooks quickly and evenly. If you don't have one, a nonstick skillet will also get the job done.

Grinder, pestle and mortar, blender, and Microplane grater

These are kitchen facilitators. They are not all essentials, but I think every self-respecting kitchen should have a blender and a Microplane grater for making large and small quantities, respectively, of pastes. Also useful is a pestle and mortar or a small spice grinder for grinding fresh spices.

Muslin or cheesecloth

This thin, light cloth is used when making paneer, traditional Indian cheese (see page 26). It is inexpensive and can be washed and reused.

Rolling pin and tongs

The rolling pin is essential for rolling out the many Indian flat breads. Tongs are really useful, not only for turning and handling bread but also for turning vegetables and meats that are broiling in the oven.

Spice container

This is a round steel container—not very attractive but really useful. It houses small, deep bowls in which you place all your most used spices so that when you are cooking, everything you need is at hand. I actually have two—one for powdered spices and one for whole. This means my cabinets are free of plastic bags of half-used and spilling spices.

Lastly, I cook using gas, rather than electricity, as I find that I have greater control when cooking and that food cooks quicker on gas. I have explained how the dishes should look and smell at the different stages, so follow these guidelines to get the recipe right, as well as following the time guide.

The Recipes Made Easy

Whenever I take things for granted or make assumptions, I get into trouble. So, when it comes to cooking a new cuisine, I assume a lack of knowledge and then look forward to learning about it. When it comes to Indian food, I have seen so many people make preventable mistakes (simple things like choosing the wrong chili or tomato) that have left their dishes less than perfect. It might be useful to have a quick read of this chapter to make sure the dishes turn out as they should and to start to understand the basics. Also have a look at the Glossary on page 156. For those of you who have already mastered the basics and are finding cookbooks repetitive, bear with me, as we're still in the early stages in this culinary evolution!

Chilies

People seem to have forgotten that chilies have a wonderful flavor. They can be really hot to eat but are not spicy as such. Remember the basic rule—the bigger the chili, the milder it is. Green chilies ripen into red ones but then have a slightly different flavor. I find the red ones slightly sweeter than the green ones, a bit like bell peppers. I often leave chilies whole in my food so that they impart flavor without too much heat, as this is contained mainly in the seeds and membranes.

If you don't have fresh chilies, dried red chilies or even chili flakes are a good substitute; they add heat as well as a little flavor. Chili powder, however, will give your food a great color and lots of heat but little flavor. The important thing to remember is that unless a recipe says otherwise, always use the long, thin green chilies that look like knobbly fingers. Other chilies will not give you the same flavor. If you bite into a harsh chili, follow with yogurt or something sweet. When handling chilies, always wash your hands afterward; if you were to wipe your eye, you'd have a painful experience!

Coconut

The coastal regions of the south and west of India tend to use the ubiquitous coconut to sweeten and to add richness and texture to their dishes. I don't always have a fresh coconut at home, so often use canned coconut milk and shredded coconut instead, as they work really well. If, however, you love coconut, buy a coconut grater, or scraper, from a well-stocked Indian shop. They are inexpensive and easy to use.

Garlic

Garlic cloves vary a lot in size—from little slivers, ¼ in. or less at the thickest part, to great fat ones, about ¾ in. thick. Unless otherwise stated, the cloves in these recipes are medium-sized: about ⅜ to ½ in. thick. If yours are smaller, or larger, adjust the number accordingly.

Ghee

This is simply clarified butter. It can be bought in some stores but is easy to make. Warm some unsalted butter in a saucepan, and cook gently until the color changes to pure gold. By this time all the milk impurities will have risen to the surface and should be removed with a spoon. The ghee is now ready to use. Store in a jar in the fridge.

Ginger

In these recipes I've measured ginger in pieces, giving the length in inches. You'll need first to peel a section and cut a roughly square-sided stick, just under ¾ in. thick. Then trim the length as required. People have often asked me where to buy ginger paste, I never realized that people actually bought pastes—they are so easy to make at home. Use a Microplane grater or a blender. You can store the paste in teaspoon-sized batches in ice-cube trays in the freezer and add them straight to the pan.

Masala

I often throw the word "masala" around, assuming everyone knows what I am talking about. I have now realized that, of course, most don't. It is one of the basic foundations of Indian food. It is, in this context, the mixture of ingredients that forms the base of most curries. It is like making a gravy or curry sauce to which you add the main ingredient. A poorly cooked masala will result in a one-dimensional dish, so take your time and cook the masala properly at each stage. To gauge if it is cooked, look for little bubbles of oil being released on the sides, and if still in doubt, try it—if there are no harsh flavors, it is properly cooked.

Meat and Poultry

The best way to get the most from your red or white meat is to cook it on the bone, as this provides that wonderful meaty flavor that we often add back in with good-quality stock (which is made from those same bones). We cook our red meat until falling off the bone—there is never any trace of pink —but I leave it to you to cook lamb how you like. If you use meat without the bones, you can either add extra bones to the dish as it cooks and fish them out later or add some stock instead of water. When cooking lamb, I usually choose shoulder or leg, but you can use cheaper cuts if a recipe requires long, slow cooking. A good butcher will prepare cubed lamb with the bone in if you ask. Also, do skin chicken joints, as we do not brown them in the pan and this can leave the cooked skin a little flabby and chewy. It would also act as a barrier, preventing the flavors of the gravy from getting into the flesh.

Onions

These are a really important ingredient in Indian food. They add depth of flavor, body, richness, and sweetness to a dish. Not all curries will have onions, but the onion masala (base of a curry/gravy) will always be used abundantly in North Indian restaurant kitchens. When cooking onions, you need to make sure that the onion is properly cooked and to the right stage. As onions cook, they absorb any oil in the pan, then once cooked they release the oil back, and you know they are done. If the recipe says the onions should be soft, they should be translucent; if golden, the softened onion should be cooked until browned on the sides and turning golden in the center. Be wary of cooking the onions over too high a heat, causing them to brown before they soften—check by pressing a piece.

Spices

Whole spices should be the first thing added to the hot oil in a pan. They take only 10–20 seconds to cook, and when they release their aroma and just start to darken, quickly add the next ingredient. Powdered spices are very delicate, so cook them over a low heat. Spices should be kept in airtight containers away from heat and sunlight (see page 8). It's always best to buy whole spices, as they keep better and retain more flavor. They take seconds to grind in a spice grinder (see page 8).

To roast spices, use a small skillet or saucepan, and dry-roast over a moderate to low heat, shaking the pan often to cook them evenly. Keep an eye on them, and pour them out of the pan as soon as they are roasted and fragrant, around 1 minute. Use a pestle and mortar to grind to a powder.

Tamarind

This is a coastal fruit that grows in papery brown pods on trees of the same name. It is an important ingredient and is used to add a sour element to many South Indian curries. It can be a bit tricky to extract the paste from the block of tamarind, but ready-made pastes are now available (check the Internet). Add judiciously, as they all have different strengths.

Tomatoes

In India tomatoes are used for their slight sourness, as well as their flavor. For Indian food, you need to buy the cheap cooking tomatoes—the ones that look unripe and flavorless. Juicy, sweet plum or vine tomatoes are great for salads and raitas but can sometimes be too sweet for our dishes.

Yogurt

As yogurt ages, it gets more and more sour, which is fine, as we sometimes need yogurt for its freshness and other times for its sour quality. Fresh and sweet for desserts and raitas, slightly sour for general cooking, and even very sour for some specific dishes; the recipe will always say if it should be particularly fresh or sour. If the yogurt is too fresh, you may need to add a little lemon juice at the end of the cooking. Taste and decide.

Succulent Chicken Tikka Wraps

Chili Cheese Toast

Masala Scrambled Eggs

Potato and Pea Samosas

Paneer, Mushroom, and Spinach Wraps

Paneer

Simple Semolina Pilaff

LIGHT
MEALS
and
SNACKS

Tandoori Lamb Wraps

Paneer and Vegetable Skewers

Savory Semolina Cake

Makes 8

1 lb. 2 oz. chicken breast, skinned, boned, and cut into 1-in. cubes
vegetable oil, for frying
10 wooden skewers, soaked in water for 30 minutes
2 tablespoons melted butter, to baste
8 flour tortillas
¾ teaspoon chaat masala (optional)
½ onion, 2 tomatoes, and one head of Boston lettuce, all finely sliced
½ cup cilantro and mint chutney

Marinade

⅝ cup Greek-style thick yogurt
1 tablespoon vegetable oil
1 in. fresh ginger (see page 12)
8 large garlic cloves, peeled
¼ – ½ teaspoon red chili powder, or to taste
¾ teaspoon garam masala
generous pinch of green and black cardamom seeds and fennel seeds, ground together
¾ –1 teaspoon salt, or to taste
¼ cup cheddar cheese, coarsely grated
1½ tablespoons lemon juice
1 egg
2 rounded tablespoons chickpea flour

Succulent Chicken Tikka Wraps

These easy wraps make a perfect light lunch. Don't let the cheese in the marinade throw you—this is an authentic tandoori recipe. Cheese was first introduced as a way to quieten the flavors of the original chicken tikka for the tourists, the strong flavors being replaced with more delicate spices. The result was so delicious that this has now become a standard tandoori recipe and is found across India. We often make mini versions to serve with predinner drinks, and the chicken is also great served with salad and raita.

Blend together the ingredients for the marinade and tip into a nonmetallic bowl. Pierce the chicken all over with a fork and add to the marinade. Leave to marinate in the fridge for a few hours, if possible. Bring back to room temperature before cooking.

Preheat the broiler. Brush the broiler rack liberally with oil, and place some foil below to catch any drips. Thread the chicken pieces onto the skewers, spacing them apart so they do not touch. Broil for 6 minutes (using the upper shelf if your broiler has that option), turning halfway, then baste with the butter and broil for another minute —the chicken should be slightly charred at the edges and cooked through.

Meanwhile, wrap the tortillas in foil and warm in the oven for 5 minutes while the chicken is cooking.

Using a fork, slide the chicken pieces off the skewers onto a plate and sprinkle over the chaat masala, if using. Divide the chicken into eight portions, and place each in the middle of a warmed tortilla, top with the vegetables, and spoon 1½–2 tablespoons of the chutney over. Fold over the top of the tortilla, pull in the sides, and continue wrapping. Cut the wrap in half on the diagonal. Repeat with the remaining tortillas and serve.

Serves 6

14 oz. boned lamb, cut into ¾-in. cubes and pierced with a fork
10 wooden skewers, soaked in water for 30 minutes
2 tablespoons melted butter, for basting
6 flour tortillas
sliced onions, lettuce, and sliced tomatoes, to serve
⅓ cup green chutney (see page 134) mixed with 3 tablespoons yogurt, to serve

Marinade

⅝ cup Greek-style thick yogurt
½ small onion, peeled and roughly chopped
8 large garlic cloves, peeled
1 in. fresh ginger (see page 12)
1½ teaspoons garam masala
1½ teaspoons ground cumin
1 teaspoon ground coriander
½ teaspoon fennel seeds, ground
¼ teaspoon freshly ground black peppercorns
1 tablespoon vegetable oil
2 tablespoons fresh cilantro leaves
½ teaspoon red chili powder, or to taste
2 teaspoons lemon juice
1 teaspoon salt, or to taste

Tandoori Lamb Wraps

These wraps are the perfect grab-and-go meal. You can prepare the ingredients well in advance and simply broil the lamb in the time it takes you to slice the tomato and onion. The chutney also keeps well in the fridge for a few days. The flavors are clean and deep and the textures varied. You can also use seasoned yogurt and some chopped fresh cilantro and mint instead of the chutney.

Blend all the marinade ingredients until smooth. Pour into a nonmetallic bowl, mix in the lamb, and leave to marinate for as long as possible—overnight in the fridge would be best. Bring back to room temperature before cooking.

Preheat the broiler. Thread the lamb onto the skewers, leaving a space between each piece, and place under the broiler. Cook for 5–6 minutes until tender, turning halfway through cooking. Alternatively, cook in an oven preheated to 400°F for 8 minutes. Baste with the butter and cook another minute or two for slightly pink meat (or for slightly longer if you prefer meat well done).

Wrap the tortillas in foil and warm in the oven for the last 5 minutes of the cooking time.

Divide the lamb into six portions and place in the center of the warmed tortillas. Top with some of the vegetables and spoon 1½ tablespoons of green chutney over (see page 134). Roll and serve.

Serves 5

Marinade

⅓ cup Greek-style thick yogurt
¾ teaspoon each garam masala,
    ground cumin, fennel, and green
    cardamom powder
2 teaspoons garlic paste
1 rounded teaspoon ginger paste
2 teaspoons chickpea flour
salt, to taste
2 teaspoons lemon juice
¼ – ½ teaspoon red chili powder,
    or to taste
2 teaspoons vegetable oil
2 tablespoons water

7 oz. portobello mushrooms
6 wooden skewers, soaked in water for
    30 minutes
10–12 oz. paneer, or to taste (see
    page 26), cut into 1-in. cubes
2 tablespoons vegetable oil, for frying,
    plus extra for oiling pan
scant ½ cup water
½ small onion, peeled and thinly sliced
5 flour tortillas

Spinach paste

2 cups baby spinach leaves, washed
3 handfuls fresh cilantro, leaves and
    stalks
6 large garlic cloves, peeled
2 in. fresh ginger (see page 12), roughly
    chopped
6 tablespoons roasted and salted peanuts
2–3 tablespoons lemon juice, or to taste
1 tablespoon vegetable oil
salt and freshly ground black pepper
1–3 green chilies (optional)

Paneer, Mushroom, and Spinach Wraps

This vegetarian wrap has enough flavors and textures to please all palates. The tandoori mushrooms add meatiness and depth of flavor, and the paneer adds freshness, while the spinach paste brings all the flavors together. If you don't have time to make all the different elements, the wrap works just as well without the mushrooms or without the paneer; the spinach paste is the only essential ingredient.

Clean the mushrooms, then boil them in water for 15 minutes. Drain and leave to cool, then slice thickly.

Blend all the marinade ingredients to a smooth paste and tip into a nonmetallic bowl. Add the mushrooms to the marinade and leave for 20 minutes.

Preheat the oven to 400°F and oil a roasting pan. Thread the mushrooms, well-coated in the marinade, onto the skewers, and bake in the oven for 20 minutes, turning halfway. Once cooked, add to a bowl with the paneer.

Blend all the ingredients for the spinach paste to a smooth paste. Heat the oil in a large nonstick saucepan or skillet, and add the spinach paste and the water. Cook over a moderate heat for about 15 minutes, until it starts to thicken and become smooth and creamy. Add the paneer, mushrooms, and onion, and cook for another minute or until the onion just starts to wilt.

Meanwhile, wrap the tortillas in foil and warm in the oven for a few minutes. Divide the filling into five portions and wrap each in one of the tortillas. Roll up and cut in half on the diagonal.

Chili Cheese Toast

Makes 2

1/2 cup grated cheddar cheese or your
   preferred cheese
1 scant teaspoon minced onion
1/2 small tomato, minced
1/4 teaspoon finely sliced green chilies
1 teaspoon minced fresh cilantro
2 slices of bread

We all already love cheese on toast, but once you start eating this version, it becomes very hard to revert to the simpler one. Add as much chili as you want, or, if you are really nervous, leave it out completely —it is still the best cheese on toast around.

Preheat the oven to 400°F. Mix together all the ingredients except the bread. Pile the mixture evenly on top of the bread, and bake in the oven for a couple of minutes until crisp and browning on the sides. Serve hot.

Opposite: *Chili Cheese Toast*

Masala Scrambled Eggs

Serves 1

1 teaspoon vegetable oil
1 scant teaspoon butter
1/4 small onion, peeled and minced
2 eggs
1/2 small tomato, minced
1/2 green chili, finely sliced
1 heaped tablespoon chopped fresh
   cilantro
salt, to taste

This is a quick concoction that I eat for breakfast at least twice a week. This simple dish shows that Indian food is not all spices and heat. There are no spices in this dish—just good flavors and a little sliced green chili for punch. Once you start to eat eggs cooked in this way, it is difficult to enjoy them plain.

Heat the oil and butter in a nonstick skillet. Add the onion and cook for 2 minutes.

Meanwhile, whisk the eggs with the tomato, chili, cilantro, and salt. Add the eggs to the pan, and scramble as you would normally, leaving them a little longer than usual.

Simple Semolina Pilaff

Serves 1

1 tablespoon vegetable oil
1/3 teaspoon mustard seeds
1/3 teaspoon chickpea flour
3 tablespoons chopped onion
1/2 green chili, finely sliced
handful of frozen peas
salt, to taste
scant 1/3 cup semolina
8 curry leaves
1/2 cup water

This light and nourishing pilaff, made with semolina, rather than rice, is often eaten for breakfast. It is a mild dish that can be eaten by all—I feed it to my young daughter, making it with milk rather than water and omitting the chilies, for a nutritious, calcium-packed dish. You can add more vegetables to this recipe if you wish.

Heat the oil in a nonstick saucepan. Add the mustard seeds and flour and cook until the flour starts to brown. Stir in the onion, chili, peas, and salt, and cook until the onions are translucent, then add a splash of water to cook the peas.

When soft, cook off the water. Add the semolina and curry leaves, and stir-fry over a high heat for a minute or two or until you can smell their distinctive aroma. Add the water and continue cooking and stirring until it comes together or until you can smell the semolina. Serve hot.

3 tablespoons vegetable oil, plus extra
    for oiling
1 cup semolina
generous ½ cup plain yogurt
generous ½ cup water
generous ¼ cup frozen peas
2 tablespoons chopped onion
1 small carrot, peeled and grated
handful of frozen or fresh green beans,
    roughly broken up
1 in. fresh ginger (see page 12),
    pounded into a paste
¼ – 1 teaspoon red chili powder, or
    to taste
½ teaspoon turmeric
salt, to taste (season well)
1 teaspoon mustard seeds
½ teaspoon cumin seeds
½ teaspoon baking soda
1 teaspoon sesame seeds

Savory Semolina Cake

This savory cake, known as handvo, is spongy on the inside, crisp on the edges, and replete with the textures of a variety of vegetables. It is light, satisfying, and easy to make. It hails from the Gujarati community, but this is my cheat's version—no soaking or grinding required, so purists beware! Use any vegetables you have—either those listed here or experiment with zucchini, cabbage, spinach, or fresh fenugreek leaves.

Preheat the oven to 400°F and oil a large bread pan.

Mix together the semolina, yogurt, water, vegetables, ginger, spices, and salt to make a batter of a medium–thick consistency. If it is too thick, add a splash of water. Taste and adjust the seasoning if necessary.

Heat the oil in a small saucepan. Add the mustard and cumin seeds, and cook for about 20 seconds until the mustard seeds have popped and the cumin is aromatic. Stir into the batter.

Stir in the baking soda, and immediately pour the mixture into the prepared pan and sprinkle the sesame seeds over. Bake in the preheated oven for 35–40 minutes. The cake is ready when a toothpick inserted into the center comes out clean and when the edges are crisp. Leave the cake to cool in the pan.

4 cups whole milk
⅞–1 cup fresh yogurt or
    2 tablespoons lemon juice

Paneer

Paneer is homemade, unsalted white cheese. It has all the taste of a fresh farmer's cheese and a dense, crumbly texture, which works wonderfully either combined with the spices of India or served simply with flaky coarse salt, freshly ground black pepper, and a drizzle of good-quality olive oil. Paneer is a good source of protein and is packed with vitamins and minerals. You can now buy it ready-made from some grocery stores, but as this recipe shows, it is really easy to make your own. Paneer forms the main ingredient in several dishes in this book (for example, see pages 20, 29, and 98).

Bring the milk to a boil in a heavy-based saucepan. Once the milk starts to boil and rise up, stir in ⅞ cup of the yogurt or all the lemon juice. Keeping the milk on the heat, stir gently to help the milk curdle—this should take only a minute or so. If it does not separate, add the rest of the yogurt (if using) and keep stirring. The curds will coagulate and separate from the watery whey. Remove from the heat.

Line a large strainer with muslin or cheesecloth, and place it over a large bowl or saucepan. Pour the cheese into the lined strainer and run some cold water through it. Wrap the cheese in the cloth, and hang it from the faucet over the sink to allow the excess water to drain for 10 minutes. Then, keeping it fairly tightly wrapped, place on your work surface with a heavy weight on top (I refill the same saucepan with the whey or water and place it on top) for 30–40 minutes or until it is flattened into a firm block. Then cut into cubes or crumble, depending how you want to use it.

Store any unused pieces of paneer in the refrigerator in water in a covered container. You can also freeze it in an airtight container. Defrost thoroughly before use.

Makes 6 skewers

11 oz. paneer (see page 26), cut into
  1-in. cubes
1 large onion, peeled and cut into
  1-in. cubes
1 green and 1 red bell pepper, cored
  and cut into 1-in. cubes
vegetable oil, for greasing
6 wooden skewers, soaked in water for
  1 hour
2 tablespoons melted butter
chaat masala, to sprinkle

Marinade

½ cup Greek-style yogurt
¾ in. fresh ginger (see page 12)
3 large garlic cloves, peeled
salt, to taste
¼ – ½ teaspoon chili powder, or to taste
1 teaspoon garam masala
2 tablespoons lemon juice, or to taste
2 tablespoons vegetable oil
1 tablespoon chickpea flour
1 teaspoon ground cumin
seeds of 6 green cardamom pods,
  powdered with a pestle and mortar

Paneer and Vegetable Skewers

We will be forever indebted to the northwest of India for the introduction of tandoori food. My father remembers how most homes in his town had their own small tandoor ovens to cook bread in. Now that tandoori-style food is cooked all over the world, the actual tandoor is often incidental and found mainly in restaurants—it is the flavors that we crave, however they are created. This is my vegetarian tandoori recipe. It is full flavored, has lots of texture, and is very satisfying, regardless of whether you are a vegetarian or not. Tandoori food is often served with sliced or chopped tomatoes, red onions, and cucumbers seasoned and drizzled with lemon juice, and some green chutney (see page 134).

Purée all the marinade ingredients until smooth, then place in a nonmetallic bowl. Add the paneer and vegetables, and allow them to soak up the flavors for 30–40 minutes or longer in the fridge.

Heat the broiler to a high setting, and oil a roasting pan liberally.

Thread the vegetables and paneer alternately onto the skewers. Broil for 7 minutes, drizzle the melted butter over, turn, and cook for another 2–4 minutes or until charred at the edges. Alternatively, cook in an oven preheated to 400°F for 8–10 minutes, turning halfway through. Sprinkle the skewers liberally with chaat masala and serve with bread.

3 tablespoons vegetable oil
$\frac{1}{2}$ teaspoon mustard seeds
$\frac{1}{2}$ cup chopped onion
$\frac{3}{4}$ in. fresh ginger (see page 12), minced
$\frac{3}{8}$ cup frozen peas
1 tablespoon ground coriander
1 teaspoon ground cumin
$\frac{1}{4}$ teaspoon red chili powder
$\frac{1}{2} - \frac{3}{4}$ teaspoon garam masala
1–2 teaspoons dried mango powder
salt, to taste
1 lb. 5 oz. potatoes, boiled until soft,
   peeled and crushed into large lumps
4 tablespoons chopped cilantro leaves
approximately 10 oz. phyllo pastry
5 tablespoons melted butter, for brushing
2 tablespoons sesame seeds (optional; you
   can also use poppy or nigella seeds)

Potato and Pea Samosas

This samosa recipe is simplified by using store-bought phyllo pastry, which gives a light and crisp covering, instead of the heavier chickpea-flour dough traditionally used. The filling is delicious, with a mixture of sweet, spicy, tart, and buttery flavors in each mouthful. Indian teatime snacks tend to be vegetarian, but we always have a batch of mini cocktail samosas made with ground lamb in the freezer for unexpected guests, to be served with drinks to whet their appetites. Serve with green or tamarind chutney (see pages 134 and 135).

Heat the oil in a small nonstick saucepan, and fry the mustard seeds for about 10 seconds until they splutter. Add the onion and ginger, and cook for 2 minutes over a high heat. Add the peas and give the pan a good stir, then add the spices, salt, and a splash of water. Cook for 1 minute, then add the potatoes and ground coriander, and cook for 2–3 minutes. Taste and adjust seasoning.

Preheat the oven to 400°F. Unroll the pastry, peel off one piece, then cover the remainder with plastic wrap and a damp dish towel to prevent it from drying out. Lay the first piece of pastry flat on a clean surface, and brush with melted butter. Fold in one-third of the pastry lengthwise. Brush again with the butter, and fold in the other end to make a long triple-layered strip. Halve the strip crosswise—your strip needs to be only about 4 in. long.

Place one rounded teaspoon of the filling at one of the short ends of the strip, leaving a $\frac{3}{4}$-in. border. Fold the right corner diagonally to the left, enclosing the filling and forming a triangle. Fold again along the upper crease of the triangle. Keep folding this way until you reach the end of the strip. Brush the outer surface with the butter. Place on a baking sheet and cover while you make the rest of the samosas. Before baking, sprinkle with sesame seeds, if using. Bake in the center of the oven for 30–35 minutes until golden and crisp, turning halfway through. Serve with green or tamarind chutney.

Chicken in Creamy **Yogurt**

Chili

Oven-fried Chili Chicken

Goan Coconut Chicken Curry

My Chicken **Korma**

Chicken with **Peppercorns**
and Shredded Ginger

Chicken Burgers

CHICKEN

Green Cilantro Chicken

Mangalorean Chicken

Classic Northern Chicken Curry

Serves 6–8

2-lb. 14-oz. chicken, skinned and
    jointed into small pieces
2 tablespoons vegetable oil
1 small onion, peeled and chopped
1–2 green chilies, slit (optional)
1 large or 2 small black cardamom pods
handful of fresh cilantro stalks and
    leaves, minced

Marinade

7 large garlic cloves, peeled
2½ in. fresh ginger (see page 12),
    peeled
1¾ cups plain yogurt
4 teaspoons ground coriander
½–1 teaspoon red chili powder
1 rounded teaspoon garam masala
2 teaspoons salt, or to taste
½ teaspoon ground cumin

Chicken in Creamy Yogurt

This is a delicious dish whose simplicity belies its full flavor. The recipe has been in my family for as long as I can remember, and it has always been a firm favorite of mine. It is easy to cook and can be made with the minimum of spices and even less effort. As a bonus for the health-conscious among you, very little oil is used in the dish, which simply relies on good-quality chicken and fresh yogurt for its wonderful depth of flavor and creaminess. I like to serve the chicken with some green vegetables, roti, or naan.

Purée the garlic and ginger with some of the yogurt to make a smooth paste, then stir in the remaining marinade ingredients. Tip into a nonmetallic bowl, add the chicken, and leave to marinate in the fridge for as long as possible (I leave mine overnight). Bring back to room temperature before cooking.

Pour the chicken and the marinade into a large saucepan and place over a high heat.

Meanwhile, heat the oil in a small pan and fry the onion and chilies, if using, for about 6 minutes or until soft. Once done, add to the chicken along with the cardamom pods, and continue cooking over a high heat for about 15–20 minutes until the watery curry becomes creamy and covers only one-third of the chicken.

Cover the pan and cook the chicken over a very low heat for another 10–15 minutes until it is tender and the gravy is rich and creamy. Stir occasionally, making sure there is enough water in the pan and adding a splash more if necessary. Stir in the cilantro, check the seasoning, and serve.

Serves 4–6

6 tablespoons shredded coconut
1–2 fresh large red chilies
1 in. fresh ginger (see page 12), peeled
5 large garlic cloves, peeled
½ tablespoon cumin seeds
1 teaspoon coriander seeds
2 teaspoons poppy seeds,
    preferably white

1½ tablespoons vegetable oil
1 small–medium onion, peeled and
    sliced
salt, to taste
2-lb. 2-oz. chicken, skinned and cut
    into small joints
1 cup coconut milk
2 teaspoons tamarind paste, or
    to taste
⅓ cup creamed coconut

Goan Coconut Chicken Curry

This creamy curry is typical Goan fare. It is a mild dish that is full of flavor. The triple dose of coconut is not a statement but an easy substitute for fresh coconut, which can be cumbersome to deal with. In an ideal world, one coconut would be cracked open, some flesh ground with water to get thick milk, some ground for thin milk, and the remainder grated. I find it easier to substitute three store-bought alternatives, but you can use the real thing if you prefer. Goans often eat their curries with their local bread or with red, nutty rice. I think it works well with any rice, naan, or even French bread.

Dry-roast the coconut in a small pan over a medium heat until it is golden brown. Grind into a fine paste with the red chilies, ginger, garlic, cumin, coriander, and poppy seeds. Add a splash of water to help it grind down.

Heat the oil in a nonstick saucepan. Add the onion and fry for 4–5 minutes until it is golden brown. Add the salt and paste, and fry for another 5–6 minutes or until all the excess moisture has dried off and the paste has had a few minutes to fry off.

Add the chicken pieces and cook in the paste for 5 minutes over a moderate heat, then stir in the coconut milk and bring to a gentle boil. Turn the heat down to low, and cook, covered, for 30–35 minutes or until the chicken is cooked through.

Uncover the pan and stir in the tamarind and creamed coconut; cook for another few minutes or until the gravy is creamy. If there is not enough water in the pan at any time, add a splash or two of recently boiled water.

Serves 6

1¾ lb. chicken joints, skinned and
    forked all over
3 tablespoons vegetable oil
¼ teaspoon salt
¼ teaspoon freshly ground black pepper
¾ teaspoon ground cumin
4 slices of white bread, crumbed
1 large egg, beaten
1 lemon, cut into wedges, to serve

Marinade

1¼ in. fresh ginger (see page 12),
    roughly chopped
9 large garlic cloves, peeled
2–4 green chilies, seeds and
    membranes removed (optional)
1 teaspoon salt, or to taste
1 teaspoon garam masala
1 tablespoon lemon juice
2 tablespoons vegetable oil

Oven-fried Chili Chicken

These delicious joints of chicken are crisp on the outside and juicy on the inside.
They are my idea of perfect sharing food, especially if men and TV are involved. The
flavors are clean and simple, and the cooking process is easy. I like to serve these
fresh from the oven, so all I do is throw them in when my friends are having their first
drink, and they are ready just in time. The green chili is hot, but it is the flavor that
is really important here, so scrape out the seeds and cut off the membranes, if you
wish, to minimize the heat.

Blend all the marinade ingredients into a paste, and place in a nonmetallic bowl. Add the chicken and coat well
in the paste. Leave in the fridge to marinate for a couple of hours or overnight. Bring back to room temperature
before cooking.

Preheat the oven to 425°F. Pour the oil into a roasting pan large enough to accommodate the chicken in one
open layer. Place the pan on a high shelf in the oven to heat up for 15 minutes.

Mix the salt, black pepper, and ground cumin into the breadcrumbs. Take the chicken out of the marinade, letting
the excess drip off, and roll in the spicy crumbs, ensuring an even coating on all sides. Dip into the egg and add
a second coating of crumbs.

Place the chicken in the oiled roasting pan and cook for 20 minutes. Then lower the oven temperature to 400°F,
turn the chicken over, and cook for another 15–25 minutes (depending on the size of the joints) or until cooked
through. Serve with lemon wedges.

Serves 4

1½ lb. bone-in small chicken joints, skinned and cleaned
2 tablespoons vegetable oil or ghee
10 black peppercorns
10 green cardamom pods
1 black cardamom pod
10 cloves
1 small stick of cinnamon
1 piece of mace
1–2 green chilies, left whole
salt and freshly ground black pepper, to taste
1 medium onion, peeled and chopped
⅞ cup water
generous ½ cup creamed coconut
3 tablespoons ground almonds
¾ teaspoon garam masala
good pinch of sugar
handful of fresh cilantro leaves and stalks, chopped

Marinade

⅞ cup plain yogurt
1 heaped tablespoon garlic paste
1 heaped tablespoon ginger paste
2 teaspoons ground coriander

My Chicken Korma

"Korma" is the name given to any pale, creamy curry. It can be made with yogurt, cream, nut and seed pastes, and coconut—there don't seem to be any rules. I associate korma dishes with the tables of the Mogul royalty. It is usually quite rich but more delicate than many other curries. There is normally a little fried and ground coconut added to the dish, but, because I wouldn't go to the trouble of extracting the flesh from a coconut for such a small quantity, I opt for creamed coconut. In this recipe I have tried to restrain my use of the heavier dairy products, but if you wish you can replace some of the yogurt in the marinade with cream. I think this curry is delicious, and it's really quick and easy to make.

Mix the marinade ingredients together in a nonmetallic bowl, add the chicken, stir, and marinate for at least 30 minutes or for as long as possible. Cover and put in the fridge, if you have the time to leave it longer. Bring back to room temperature before cooking.

Heat the oil in a large nonstick pan, and add the whole spices, give the pan a good stir, and add the onion, green chilies, and salt. Fry for about 6 minutes until the onions are golden. Add the chicken along with the marinade and the water. Turn the heat up and bring to the boil, then simmer, covered, over a lowish heat for about 25–35 minutes, depending on the size of the joints, until the chicken is tender, stirring every now and then. Add a splash of water if the pan is getting dry at any stage. Stir in the coconut and almonds, and cook, uncovered, for another 3 minutes until the gravy is creamy.

Add the garam masala, sugar, and fresh cilantro, taste, and adjust seasoning. Serve with rice or roti.

Serves 6

1 tablespoon vegetable oil
½ medium onion, peeled and chopped
2-lb. 2-oz. chicken, skinned and cut into
    small joints
1 cup water
salt, to taste
1 tablespoon butter
1 tablespoon lemon juice, or to taste

Paste

12 cups fresh cilantro stalks
1 medium onion, peeled and quartered
1–2 green chilies, halved
7 large garlic cloves, peeled
1½ in. fresh ginger (see page 12)
12 black peppercorns
1 teaspoon coriander seeds
1 teaspoon cumin seeds
1 tablespoon poppy seeds, preferably
    white
2 cloves
1 small stick of cinnamon
6 green cardamom pods

Green Cilantro Chicken

For me, the color green, when linked to food, means freshness and herby undernotes. This is a delicious light and summery dish in which the cilantro is used more for taste, than for fragrance or texture.

Blend together the ingredients for the paste, reserving a small handful of cilantro.

Heat the oil in a nonstick saucepan, and fry the onion until soft and beginning to brown. Add the paste and cook for 10 minutes, stirring often, over a moderate to high heat, adding a splash of water if necessary. Then stir in the chicken, water, salt, and butter, and bring to a boil. Cover and cook over a low heat until the chicken is cooked, around 25–35 minutes.

Uncover and cook off all the extra water in the pan over a high heat, stirring often. Then adjust the seasoning and stir in the lemon juice. Chop the reserved cilantro and stir in. Serve with any flat bread or rice.

Serves 6–8

4 tablespoons vegetable oil
7 cloves
3 small sticks of cinnamon
7 green cardamom pods
2 small–medium onions, peeled and
    minced
3 tablespoons minced fresh ginger
9 large garlic cloves, peeled and minced
salt, to taste
1 teaspoon turmeric
1 teaspoon red chili powder
2 scant tablespoons ground coriander
4 medium cooking tomatoes, puréed
2-lb. chicken, skinned and jointed
3 cups water, or more if needed
1 teaspoon garam masala
handful of fresh cilantro leaves

Classic Northern Chicken Curry

To Indians, a curry simply implies a gravied dish. The actual flavors will reflect the region from which it comes. This recipe is from Punjab, and for an Indian this would be enough of a description. We know to expect the robust flavors of onions, tomatoes, ginger, garlic, and garam masala. In the old days, when I was still living at home, a night out generally ended with my girlfriends coming back to my place and ransacking the fridge to find leftovers of this curry (for some unknown reason there was always, always some sitting around). We would then polish off every last scrap with rounds of hot buttered toast to mop up the flavorful gravy as we meticulously dissected the evening's events as only women can.

Heat the oil in a large nonstick saucepan. Add the whole spices and fry for about 20 seconds until aromatic. Add the onion and cook over a moderate heat for about 10 minutes until a rich golden brown, stirring often.

Stir in the ginger and garlic, and cook for another 40 seconds, then add the salt and powdered spices; stir for another 10 seconds. Pour in the tomatoes and cook over a moderate heat for about 10 minutes until the liquid in the pan has dried off and the oil leaves the sides of the dry masala.

Add the chicken and brown over moderate to high heat for 3–4 minutes. Add enough water to almost cover the chicken, bring to a boil, and then cook over a slow to moderate heat until the chicken is cooked through. The slower it cooks, the better it tastes. This takes about 15–20 minutes for small joints and up to 25–30 minutes for larger ones.

Stir in the garam masala and cilantro leaves just before serving.

Makes 4

Burgers

14 oz. ground chicken
¾ in. ginger (see page 12), finely
    chopped
3 large garlic cloves, peeled and minced
1 small onion, peeled, half minced (for
    the burgers) and half sliced into
    rings (for serving)
large handful of fresh cilantro leaves
    and stalks, finely chopped
1 heaped teaspoon salt
¾ teaspoon garam masala
1½ slices of medium-sliced bread,
    crumbed
1 egg
1 teaspoon ground cumin
1 teaspoon lemon juice
1–2 green chilies (optional), chopped
    and seeded
1 tablespoon vegetable oil, plus extra
    for oiling the pan

To serve

scant ½ cup light mayonnaise
2 tablespoons chopped fresh cilantro
    leaves
2 teaspoons chopped fresh mint leaves
1–2 teaspoons lemon juice, or to taste
salt, to taste
¼ – ½ teaspoon black pepper, or to
    taste
4 burger buns, halved
lettuce leaves, shredded
1 beefsteak tomato, sliced

Chicken Burgers

Although a burger is obviously not of Indian origin, small, succulent chicken burgerlike kabobs are often served as appetizers with drinks. For a more substantial snack, they are sometimes wrapped in a huge handkerchief-like thin bread with sliced onions, tomatoes, and herb chutney. This recipe just involves a different choice of bread, it works beautifully, and the flavors are still Indian. You can leave out the chilies when making them for children and stir them in before cooking up a batch for yourselves. Also, some may still want the taste of ketchup instead of the chutney-flavored mayo.

Mix together the ingredients for the burgers, leaving out the onion rings. Allow the mixture to rest for 10 minutes in the fridge. Preheat the oven to 400°F.

Mold the chicken into four burgers and place on an oiled baking sheet. Place in the oven and cook for 10 minutes, turning halfway through the cooking time.

Meanwhile, mix the mayonnaise with the cilantro and mint leaves, lemon, salt, and pepper. Warm the burger buns in the oven for the final 2 minutes of cooking time.

Place a small handful of the lettuce on the bottom of each bun with the sliced tomato and onion rings and a good dollop of the herbed mayonnaise. Top with the hot burgers and finish with the top half of the bun.

4 tablespoons shredded coconut
1 tablespoon coriander seeds
2 small sticks of cinnamon
5 cloves
10 black peppercorns
1 tablespoon poppy seeds
5 large garlic cloves, peeled
¾ in. fresh ginger (see page 12)
1 medium onion, peeled and quartered,
    and ½ small onion, peeled and
    chopped
1–3 large fat red chilies, to taste
1¾ cups water
2 tablespoons vegetable oil
salt, to taste
1½ lb. chicken joints, skinned and
    jointed
3 tomatoes, cut into wedges
handful of fresh cilantro stalks
    and leaves

Mangalorean Chicken

This dish is not as spicy as the ingredients suggest—it's really well rounded and (if you use just one chili) quite mild. The coconut reminds you of its coastal provenance, and the red chilies are typical of Mangalorean cuisine. They love their food hot! So if you want the authentic dish, use two or even three chilies. However, be aware that different varieties, and even batches, of chilies have different strengths, so use them judiciously.

Toast the coconut in a dry pan until it is golden. In a bowl, mix together the toasted coconut, coriander seeds, cinnamon, cloves, peppercorns, poppy seeds, garlic, ginger, the quartered onion, red chilies, and ⅚ cup of the water to form a paste.

Heat the oil in a nonstick saucepan, add the chopped onion, and fry until browned. Add the paste and salt, and cook for 10 minutes over a moderate to high heat, adding a splash of water if necessary. Add the chicken and tomatoes, and cook until the tomatoes have softened, then add the remaining water. Bring to a boil, then lower the heat and simmer, covered, for 25–35 minutes until the chicken is cooked.

When the chicken is cooked, uncover and reduce the excess water in the pan over a high heat, stirring often. Stir in the cilantro and adjust the seasoning before serving.

Serves 6

2 lb. 2 oz. chicken joints, skinned, with all visible fat removed
3 tablespoons vegetable oil
1 small onion, peeled and minced
1–2 green chilies, to taste
2 in. fresh ginger (see page 12) sliced into thin shreds
1 tablespoon ground coriander
salt, to taste
1 cup water
1 tablespoon black peppercorns, coarsely ground, or to taste
$^1/_2$ teaspoon garam masala
2 teaspoons lemon juice
2 handfuls of chopped fresh cilantro leaves and stalks

Marinade

10 large garlic cloves, peeled
$1^1/_2$ in. fresh ginger (see page 12)
1 teaspoon garam masala
1 chicken stock cube, dissolved in 3 tablespoons hot water

Chicken with Peppercorns and Shredded Ginger

This dish is one of our family basics, and whenever certain friends came over for dinner they hoped—nay, almost asked in advance —for this dish. I soon anticipated the question and made it almost to order. The predominant flavors of this dish are the freshly ground black pepper, ginger, and cilantro. All the other ingredients round off these clean and intense flavors. Really, truly delicious.

Make a paste with the garlic, ginger, garam masala, and chicken stock. Tip into a nonmetallic bowl, add the chicken, stir to coat well, and marinate in the fridge for at least 1 hour or for as long as possible. Return to room temperature before cooking.

Heat the oil in a nonstick saucepan. Add the onion and sauté for about 8 minutes or until brown. Add the green chilies, ginger, ground coriander, and salt, and cook for 30–40 seconds.

Add the chicken with the marinade and sear on all sides, about 3–4 minutes. Add the water and black pepper, and bring to a boil. Then lower the heat, cover, and simmer for 20–30 minutes until the chicken is tender. Stir the pan occasionally, adding splashes of hot water if necessary.

Increase the heat and stir the chicken for at least 3–4 minutes to reduce the gravy to just a few tablespoons. Stir in the garam masala, lemon juice, and cilantro just before serving.

Himalayan Lamb
and Yogurt Curry

Dry Coconut Lamb

Curried Lamb Meatballs

North Indian
Lamb Curry

Honey-roasted Spicy Leg of Lamb

MEAT

Herby Lamb Chops

Lamb with Squat Green Chilies

Lamb Burgers with Herbed Yogurt

Easy All-in-one Lamb Curry

2 bay leaves
¾ teaspoon ground ginger
2 black cardamom pods
2 small sticks of cinnamon
8 small cloves
10 green cardamom pods
1 piece of mace
¾ teaspoon salt
12 black peppercorns, lightly pounded
4 good teaspoons ground fennel seeds
1 lb. 5 oz. lamb, cubed with the bone in
1 cup water
1¼ cups plain yogurt
2 tablespoons oil or ghee
¾ teaspoon garam masala
salt, to taste

Himalayan Lamb and Yogurt Curry

This is a really unusual, clean, mild, and fragrant curry from Kashmir. It is so different from most people's perception of Indian food that it is worth trying just to understand the diversity of Indian flavor combinations. The dish is typical of this region in that it has no onions or garlic, and ginger is in powdered form. The flavor is provided entirely by the spices, yogurt, and meat, and for this reason, all should be good quality, and the meat should be cooked on the bone, as this provides much of the lamb's flavor. As a bonus, there is no chopping. Serve with simple boiled rice.

Place the bay leaves, ginger, black cardamom pods, cinnamon, half the cloves, half the green cardamom pods, mace, salt, peppercorns, and 3 teaspoons of the ground fennel seeds in a nonstick saucepan, along with the meat and the water. Bring to a boil, then cover and cook on a low heat for about 35 minutes until the meat is tender.

Stir in the yogurt and bring to a gentle simmer, then cook on a low heat for another 10 minutes. Add a splash of recently boiled water if necessary.

Meanwhile, heat the oil or ghee in a small pan, and add the remaining cloves and cardamom pods, cook for 20 seconds, and stir into the meat with the garam masala and remaining ground fennel seeds. Check the seasoning and serve with plain boiled rice.

The dish has a pale, thin, flavorful, and aromatic gravy, which is delicious with rice or Indian bread. If the gravy has reduced too much, add a little recently boiled water.

Serves 4

1 medium–large onion, peeled and
  minced
3 tablespoons vegetable oil
2 bay leaves
1 small stick of cinnamon
2½ medium cooking tomatoes
1 in. fresh ginger (see page 12)
3 large garlic cloves, peeled
3½ cups water
½ teaspoon turmeric
¼ – ¾ teaspoon red chili powder, or
  to taste
2 teaspoons ground coriander
1 teaspoon garam masala
salt, to taste
good handful of fresh cilantro stalks
  and leaves, chopped

Meatballs

1¾ lb. ground lamb
2 tablespoons finely chopped fresh
  cilantro leaves and stalks
¾ teaspoon garam masala
1 teaspoon minced ginger
3 garlic cloves, peeled and minced
1 large egg
½ teaspoon salt

Curried Lamb Meatballs

This delicious curry, with its light, floating meatballs, was one of my favorite childhood dishes. It conjures up memories of a pot of bubbling gravy with each bursting bubble releasing the fragrant scent of a well-blended and perfectly cooked masala. Without the chili, this is a great dish for the whole family (add a little paprika for color). Serve with basmati rice or with buttery noodles.

Mix all the ingredients for the meatballs, adding 3 tablespoons of the chopped onion.

Heat the oil in a deep nonstick saucepan. Add the bay leaves, cinnamon, and remaining chopped onion, and fry until the onion is golden brown.

Meanwhile, purée the tomatoes, ginger, and garlic, and add to the pan. Cook over a medium heat until the oil comes to the surface, about 7–8 minutes, then add 1 cup of the water and continue cooking until all the water has evaporated. Stir-fry this paste for 3 minutes, then add the powdered spices and salt. Add the remaining water, cover, bring to a boil, and simmer for 5–6 minutes while you form walnut-sized meatballs from the lamb mixture.

Add the meatballs to the pan, cover, and simmer for 20 minutes, shaking the pan every so often; but do not stir, as the meatballs could break. Add the cilantro, shake the pan, and serve.

Serves 6–8

3 in. fresh ginger (see page 12)
10 large garlic cloves, peeled
3 tablespoons vegetable oil
2 each black and green cardamom pods
1 bay leaf
1 large onion, peeled and minced
1 ¾ lb. lamb, bone in, cut into small
    cubes
1–2 green chilies, whole (optional)
½ teaspoon turmeric
1 tablespoon ground coriander
1 teaspoon garam masala
salt, to taste
4 medium tomatoes, puréed
2 generous cups water
good handful of fresh cilantro leaves
    and stalks, chopped

North Indian Lamb Curry

This is a typical, warming dish from Punjab, and we have been making it at home for as long as I can remember. The whole cardamom pods added at the beginning of the recipe bring a wonderful depth and roundness to the flavor of the curry, but if you don't have any, don't worry—the curry is delicious, regardless. The cilantro adds a lightness and freshness to the dish, which makes it so much more than just a garnish. Eat the lamb with roti or rice pilaff or, as we sometimes did, in a hot, buttered baguette—truly delicious.

Make a paste of the ginger and garlic, adding a little water to help if you are using a blender.

Heat the oil in a large nonstick saucepan. Add the cardamom pods and bay leaf, and stir for 10 seconds, then add the onion. Fry for about 8 minutes until nicely browned. Add the lamb and stir-fry for 2–3 minutes, then add the ginger and garlic paste, the spices, and salt (and green chilies, if using). Cook, stirring, for a couple of minutes or until the pan is dry.

Add the tomatoes, bring to a boil, and simmer until the masala has cooked through, around 10–15 minutes. The oil will come out of the masala, and there should be no harshness to taste. Add the water, bring to a boil, then lower the heat and cook, covered, for 35–45 minutes until the lamb is tender. Stir occasionally, and make sure there is always some water in the pan. When cooked, stir in the cilantro, turn off the heat, and serve.

Serves 4

1½ tablespoons vegetable oil
1 medium onion, peeled and sliced
2–4 green chilies, left whole
4 lamb chops (approximately 1 lb. 5 oz.),
    trimmed of any excess fat
3 large garlic cloves, peeled and
    chopped
2 teaspoons chopped fresh ginger
1 teaspoon garam masala
salt, to taste
1 cup water
11 scant cups fresh cilantro stalks and
    leaves
4 sprigs of fresh mint, leaves only
4 tablespoons plain yogurt
lemon juice, to taste

Herby Lamb Chops

Lamb chops have lots of flavor and work wonderfully with Indian spices. Also, since we like to eat with our hands, eating messy chops actually adds to our eating pleasure. These chops are cooked simply with some basic flavorings, then have a large helping of cilantro and mint added to the gravy. These mellow with cooking, so the end result is not too herby but very aromatic and flavorful. I keep a little back to add at the end of the cooking to reintroduce the freshness that will have been sacrificed at the altar of flavor.

Heat the oil in a nonstick saucepan and fry the onion until past golden. Add chilies and the lamb chops, and brown on both sides, stirring often. Then add the garlic, ginger, and garam masala, and stir for 30 seconds.

Add the salt and water, bring to a boil, then cover and cook over a low–moderate heat for 15 minutes—the lamb should be cooked by now. Dry off all the excess water in the pan over a high heat, stirring often.

Purée 10 cups of the cilantro with the mint and yogurt. Stir into the lamb and cook for another 15 minutes over a moderate heat until there is little gravy remaining. Adjust the seasoning, chop and add the remaining cilantro, and drizzle with a little lemon juice, if necessary. Serve with flat bread.

Serves 5–6

4½–5 lb. leg of lamb
⅔ cup blanched almonds
scant ½ cup thick Greek-style yogurt
1½ tablespoons honey

Marinade

2 tablespoons vegetable oil
5 tablespoons lemon juice
2 in. fresh ginger (see page 12), roughly chopped
6 large garlic cloves, peeled and roughly chopped
1 tablespoon ground cumin
1 tablespoon ground coriander
¼ teaspoon red chili powder
1 tablespoon garam masala
salt, to taste
½ teaspoon freshly ground black pepper
2 tablespoons water

Honey-roasted Spicy Leg of Lamb

This leg of lamb is slightly spicy, lemony, and, at first bite, a little sweet. Honey and lemon make a fantastic combination, and the spices just add to it. As with all roast lamb recipes, this dish needs to marinate properly—ideally for 24 hours—and takes some time to cook, but it is, in essence, an easy dish. It is wonderful with simple roasted potatoes and a vegetable.

Blend together all the ingredients for the marinade.

Trim the lamb of the excess fat and membranes. Make deep, regular cuts all over the flesh with a short, sharp knife. Rub in the marinade, making sure you work it into the deep cuts. Place the lamb in a plastic food bag with any remaining marinade and leave in the fridge for 24 hours, if possible, or for at least 6 hours.

Blend together two-thirds of the almonds, the yogurt, and half the honey. Rub into the lamb, and ideally leave in the fridge for another 2 hours, but even 30 minutes will help. Bring to room temperature before cooking.

Preheat the oven to 425°F. Place the lamb on a rack with a roasting tray underneath. Cook for 15 minutes, then lower the heat to 350°F. Cook for 20–25 minutes per pound plus another 15 minutes, depending on how pink you like your lamb. Baste the lamb every 20–30 minutes or so with the juices that have dripped into the roasting tray.

Scatter over the remaining almonds and drizzle the remaining honey over, and roast for another 10 minutes. If you wish, check the lamb with a meat thermometer—you are looking for a temperature of 265–300°F, and the higher the temperature, the more cooked the meat.

Remove the lamb from the oven and allow it to rest for 15 minutes, covered with foil. Pour the gravy into a pitcher or gravy boat and skim off any excess fat. Carve the meat and serve the gravy on the side.

1¾ lb. lamb, bone in, cut into small
    pieces
1¼ cups plain yogurt
¾ teaspoon turmeric
1 tablespoon ginger paste
1 tablespoon garlic paste
1 teaspoon ground cumin
2 teaspoons ground coriander
1 teaspoon ground mustard seeds
    (ideally grind them yourself in a spice
    grinder)
1 heaped tablespoon poppy seeds,
    preferably white, made into a paste
    (I use a pestle and mortar and a
    splash of water)
salt, to taste
3 tablespoons vegetable oil
1 large onion, peeled and minced
1–2 green chilies, forked once
1 teaspoon garam masala
½ teaspoon freshly ground black pepper
good handful of fresh cilantro stalks
    and leaves, chopped

Easy All-in-one Lamb Curry

As with any Indian lamb dish in which the meat is cooked until tender and falling off the bone, this recipe is a lesson in slow-cooked food, but since the dish almost takes care of itself, this isn't a bother. This is a full-of-flavor yet mild curry; for a spicier version, add some whole garam masala (see below) to the hot oil before starting. I fork the chilies before adding them to prevent them from bursting in the pan.

Mix the lamb with the yogurt, turmeric, ginger and garlic pastes, cumin, ground coriander and mustard seeds, poppy seed paste, and salt. Leave to marinate in a nonmetallic bowl for as long as possible, or at least until you chop and cook the next batch of ingredients.

Heat the oil in a nonstick saucepan, add the onion and green chilies, and fry until the onions are brown, around 6–7 minutes. Add the meat and its marinade, and stir-fry over a low heat for 3 minutes. Cover and continue to cook over a low heat for 45–50 minutes or until done, giving the pot a gentle stir every now and then. If the pan is running dry, add a splash of recently boiled water.

Once tender, stir in the garam masala and black pepper; check and adjust seasoning. Make sure there is enough water in the pan for a little gravy by adding extra if necessary. Stir in the cilantro and serve.

Whole garam masala: to add a bigger punch, add 1 black cardamom pod, 4 green cardamom pods, 1 small stick of cinnamon, 3 cloves, and 1 piece of mace.

Makes 6

1 small onion, peeled
1½ in. fresh ginger (see page 12)
4 large garlic cloves, peeled
2 cups fresh cilantro stalks and leaves
2–3 green chilies, chopped, or
    ½–1 teaspoon red chili powder
1 lb. ground lamb (ground beef can also
    be used)
¾ teaspoon ground cumin
1½ teaspoons garam masala
1 rounded teaspoon salt, or to taste
1 large egg
2 slices of thickly sliced white bread,
    crumbed, or enough to bind well
2 tablespoons vegetable oil, plus extra
    for oiling

Herbed yogurt

1¼ cups Greek-style thick yogurt
3 cups fresh cilantro leaves
1 handful fresh mint leaves or
    1 tablespoon good-quality dried mint
1–2 green chilies (optional)
salt, to taste
½–1 teaspoon freshly ground black pepper

To serve

6 hamburger buns
lettuce leaves
2 plum tomatoes, sliced crosswise
1 onion, peeled and sliced crosswise
    into large rings

Lamb Burgers with Herbed Yogurt

This recipe may not sound like an overtly Indian dish, and in a way it isn't. However, it is heavily based on the traditional lamb kabobs we've been eating for hundreds of years. This is my way of incorporating the delicious flavors of these kabobs into everyday eating. The succulent burgers are packed with interesting flavors, and they work beautifully with the cool herbed yogurt and the fresh crunch of the vegetables.

Using a hand blender, mince the onion, ginger, garlic, cilantro, and green chilies by pulsing, or chop them all by hand. Add to the ground meat, along with the remaining ingredients.

Shape into six burgers and chill for 20 minutes or until you want to eat, taking them out of the fridge 30 minutes before you want to start cooking.

Meanwhile, mix together all the ingredients for the herbed yogurt, and season to taste.

Heat the oven or broiler, and cook the burgers on a well-oiled baking sheet or broiler pan for 10 minutes, turning them halfway. I like to add the hamburger buns to the oven for 3–4 minutes before I take the burgers out.

Serve in warmed hamburger buns on a bed of lettuce, tomato, and onion rings, with a good spoonful of the herbed yogurt on the top.

Serves 6

1 generous cup shredded coconut
3 tablespoons vegetable oil
2 small onions, peeled and finely sliced
1 tablespoon ginger paste
1 tablespoon garlic paste
$1/2$ teaspoon turmeric
$1/2$ teaspoon red chili powder
4 medium cooking tomatoes, chopped
salt, to taste
2 lb. lamb, bone in, cut into 1-in. pieces
$1\frac{3}{4}$ cups water
1 teaspoon garam masala

Dry Coconut Lamb

This really easy lamb dish is not a curry, as the fantastic, textured gravy is thick enough to cling to the tender meat. This dish has a depth of sweetness from the onion and the coconut, but is balanced out with the tartness from the tomatoes. Perfect with roti or naan. Leaving the meat on the bone adds flavor—you can ask your butcher to prepare the meat for you.

Dry-roast the coconut in a nonstick pan until a little past golden. Reserve.

Heat the oil in a nonstick saucepan, add the onions, and cook over a moderate heat until they are well browned. Add the ginger and garlic pastes and the turmeric and chili powder; cook for about 30 seconds, adding a splash of recently boiled water if the pan is too dry. Add the tomatoes and salt, and cook until they have broken down and the oil leaves the sides of the masala, around 10–15 minutes.

Add the lamb and brown over a moderate heat for a few minutes. Add the water, bring to a boil, then cover and simmer over a low heat for 40–50 minutes until the lamb is cooked through. If the pan is running dry at any time, add a splash of recently boiled water. Once cooked, uncover and dry off any excess water over a high heat, stirring often.

When there is only a little liquid left, stir in the garam masala. Check and adjust seasoning, then stir in the roasted coconut and serve.

Serves 6

1¾ lb. lamb, bone in, cut into small
  cubes with the bone in
3 tablespoons vegetable oil
1 teaspoon cumin seeds
½ teaspoon nigella seeds
2 cups water
5–8 fat, short green chilies, slit and
  seeds removed
2–3 teaspoons tamarind paste
2 handfuls of fresh cilantro leaves and
  stalks, chopped

Marinade

1 teaspoon turmeric
1 teaspoon fennel seed powder
1 teaspoon garam masala
1 tablespoon white poppy seeds
salt, to taste
3 large garlic cloves, peeled
2 in. fresh ginger (see page 12), roughly
  chopped
1 large onion, peeled and chopped
2 medium cooking tomatoes

Lamb with Squat Green Chilies

This is a robust dish inspired by the fare of the southern city of Hyderabad. It is spicy, bold, full of flavor, and unapologetic. The cuisine from this region is generally sophisticated, and its cooks were traditionally considered among the most talented. The fat chilies are full of that inimitable green chili flavor but without the killer bite of the smaller ones.

Blend the ingredients for the marinade until smooth, and pour into a nonmetallic bowl. Add the lamb, stir, and leave to marinate for as long as possible.

Heat 2 tablespoons of the oil, add the cumin and nigella seeds, and fry for about 30 seconds until the cumin browns. Pour in the meat and its marinade, and stir-fry over a moderate heat until the masala is cooked, around 12–14 minutes. Taste—it should have no harsh elements. Add the water and bring to a boil, then lower the heat, cover, and cook until the lamb is tender, around 35–40 minutes. Keep checking the pot for water, and give it a good stir from time to time.

Halfway through cooking the lamb, heat the remaining oil in a small pan, and gently fry the chilies for 2 minutes, stirring often. Pour into the cooking meat.

Once the lamb is cooked, uncover and stir in the tamarind paste. Taste and adjust the seasoning, add some recently boiled water or dry off any excess—you are looking for a curry that is neither watery nor dry but creamy. Stir in the cilantro, and serve with naan or rice.

Tandoori **Monkfish**

Coconut Mackerel Curry

Spiced Crab Cakes with Tamarind Mayonnaise

Simple North Indian Fish Curry

Coconut and Chili

Pan-fried Halibut

Green Fish Curry

Shrimp Balchao

Bengali Shrimp
in a Mild Coconut Gravy

FISH
and
SEAFOOD

Mussels with Dry Coconut

Bengali-style Baked Fish

Mangalorean Shrimp Curry
with Rice Dumplings

Tandoori Shrimp flavored with Mustard

Serves 4 as a light meal

1 lb. 10 oz. monkfish, cut into large
    cubes
4 wooden skewers, soaked in water
    for 1 hour
1–2 tablespoons melted butter, to baste
lemon wedges, to serve

Marinade

2 tablespoons chickpea flour
4 tablespoons Greek-style thick yogurt
1 teaspoon lemon juice
½ teaspoon each carom seeds,
    turmeric, red chili powder, and
    paprika
2 teaspoons ginger paste
1 tablespoon garlic paste
1 teaspoon garam masala
1 tablespoon vegetable oil
1 egg
salt, to taste

Tandoori Monkfish

This is a delicious, summery dish, which is perfect for serving in warmer weather, although it is eaten all year round in India as bite-size appetizers served with drinks. I think this makes a perfect light meal, and when served with a light salad (such as the Herb- and Peanut-dressed Spinach Salad on page 102), it is simple and satisfying, yet sophisticated enough to serve to any dinner guest. I have used monkfish here because it is a hearty, meaty fish that goes wonderfully with these flavors, but any firm-fleshed fish would work well.

Mix together all the ingredients for the marinade. Rub well into the fish and leave to marinate in a nonmetallic bowl in the fridge for a few hours. Bring back to room temperature before cooking.

Preheat the oven to 350°F. Thread the fish onto the skewers, place on a baking sheet, and bake for 15 minutes in the middle of the oven. Meanwhile, make the salad and dressing. Then baste the fish with the butter, place the baking sheet on a higher shelf, and cook for another 3–4 minutes. Serve with lemon wedges and salad.

3 tablespoons vegetable oil
$1/2$ teaspoon fenugreek seeds
1 teaspoon cumin seeds
25 curry leaves, torn
2 medium onions, peeled and roughly
    chopped
2 medium tomatoes, roughly chopped
5 large garlic cloves, peeled and roughly
    chopped
1 in. fresh ginger (see page 12), roughly
    chopped
1 teaspoon turmeric
$3/4$–$1^1/_2$ teaspoon red chili powder
1 tablespoon ground coriander
$1^1/_2$ cups water
1 lb.–1 lb. 2 oz. whole mackerel,
    cleaned and cut into steaks 1 in.
    thick
3–5 green chilies, left whole
$1^1/_2$ teaspoons tamarind paste, or to
    taste
1 cup coconut milk
salt, to taste

Coconut Mackerel Curry

This is a gorgeous curry from Chennai, full of flavors that are then tamed by the coconut. It is a coastal dish and proud of it. Mackerel is very popular in the south of India and is used regularly in coconut curries with tamarind to balance the flavors. Cut it into steaks, as these keep the fish together, and the bones add flavor to the gravy. Serve with rice—nothing else is needed.

Heat the oil in a large nonstick saucepan. Add the fenugreek, cumin seeds, and 10 of the curry leaves, and fry for 10 seconds. Add the onions and cook for about 6–8 minutes until golden.

Meanwhile, purée together the tomatoes, garlic, ginger, and powdered spices. Add to the pan and cook for 8–10 minutes over a high heat or until you can see little droplets of oil on the sides of the masala. Add a splash of water at any point, if necessary.

Add the water, bring to a boil and then add the fish, green chilies, and remaining curry leaves. Bring back to the boil and cook for 3–4 minutes. Stir in most of the tamarind paste, but leave a little to add later. Once the fish is cooked, add the coconut milk. Stir well, taste, and adjust the seasoning and sourness (adding the remainder of the tamarind paste, if necessary), and add more water if you prefer a thinner curry.

Serves 4

3 tablespoons vegetable oil
¼ teaspoon fenugreek seeds
4 medium cooking tomatoes, puréed
¾ teaspoon turmeric
½ – ¾ teaspoon red chili powder, or
   to taste
½ teaspoon garam masala
2 handfuls of fresh cilantro stalks
   and leaves, roughly chopped
1 lb. 5 oz. any firm white fish steaks
1¾ cups water

Masala

9 large garlic cloves, peeled
⅝ in. fresh ginger (see page 12)
¾ teaspoon ground cumin
½ teaspoon black pepper
½ teaspoon mustard seeds, ground
1 tablespoon ground coriander
salt, to taste
3 tablespoons water

Simple North Indian Fish Curry

This curry is full-flavored, tangy, and spicy—a curry made for Indians. It is unadulterated and unapologetic. Those who like their Indian food mild need not bother with this dish. It isn't that it is too hot, but it is fisherman's food straight from the village, with no onions to sweeten it and no cream or coconut to tame it. The ultimate, authentic peasant food.

Blend the masala ingredients together to make a fine paste.

Heat the oil in a large saucepan, and fry the fenugreek seeds for 10 seconds. Add the paste, and cook over a moderate heat for 8 minutes or until the oil starts to leave the sides of the pan. Add the tomatoes, turmeric, chili, garam masala, and coriander, and cook for 8–10 minutes or until the oil starts to bubble at the sides of the paste. Taste—there should be no harsh elements to the masala.

Add the fish to the pan, coat in the paste, and leave on the heat for 3 minutes, then add the water and bring to a boil. Cover and cook over a low heat for about 7 minutes or until the fish is cooked through.

2 tablespoons vegetable oil
½ teaspoon brown mustard seeds
4 cloves
6 green cardamom pods
1 large stick of cinnamon
1 small onion, peeled, half minced and
      half uncut
1¼ in. fresh ginger (see page 12),
      quartered
2 large garlic cloves, peeled
1 teaspoon ground coriander
1¼ cups coconut milk
2–4 green chilies, left whole
salt, to taste
½–1 teaspoon black pepper
¾ teaspoon garam masala
⅜ cup water
10 curry leaves
1 lb. 2 oz. salmon or firm white fish
      fillets, cut crosswise into large
      pieces
2–3 teaspoons lemon juice
3 handfuls fresh cilantro leaves and
      stalks, chopped

Green Fish Curry

This fish curry is delicate of color and flavor but absolutely beautiful. The whole spices and green chilies add background flavor but are not strong (the seeds and membranes contain the heat and are not exposed to the curry). You can use almost any firm-fleshed fish—I love it with salmon, and the pale peach and green colors are a picture on a plate. Mild enough for children to enjoy.

Heat the oil in a nonstick pan, add the whole spices, and cook for 20 seconds. Add the chopped onion and fry for about 4–5 minutes until soft.

Meanwhile, blend together the remaining uncut onion, the ginger, garlic, ground coriander, and one-third of the coconut milk to a smooth purée. Add to the pan with the whole green chilies and salt, and cook, covered, for 12–15 minutes, giving the pot an occasional stir.

Stir in the remaining coconut milk and spices, water, curry leaves, and fish. Leave to cook undisturbed for about 3–5 minutes, depending on the thickness of the fish.

Gently stir in the lemon juice and the cilantro. Check the seasoning and serve with rice.

Serves 4

3½ –4½ tablespoons vegetable oil
1 small onion, peeled and minced
1¼ in. fresh ginger (see page 12),
    minced
2 small garlic cloves, peeled and
    minced
2 teaspoons ground coriander
¼–½ teaspoon red chili powder
salt, to taste
1 teaspoon garam masala
2 tablespoons lemon juice
2 small handfuls fresh cilantro leaves
    and stalks, chopped
2½ cups prepared crab meat
1 large egg
2½ tablespoons mayonnaise
9–10 slices of thick bread, crumbed
lightly dressed soft salad leaves, to serve

Tamarind mayonnaise

⅜ cup mayonnaise
scant ¼ cup milk
salt, to taste
¼ teaspoon freshly ground black pepper
1 scant tablespoon tamarind paste, or
    to taste
handful of fresh cilantro leaves and
    stalks, chopped

Spiced Crab Cakes
with Tamarind Mayonnaise

These crab cakes are one of the few fusion dishes in my repertoire. They are absolutely divine, even served simply with a drizzle of lemon, but the peppery tamarind mayonnaise complements them wonderfully, and a lightly dressed salad makes it a lovely lunch. Add tamarind to taste, as different brands have varying levels of tartness, or use lemon juice and rind, which do the same job. The cakes are crisp but melting on the inside, so they have to be turned carefully. The tamarind mayo is rich, so a little goes a long way (you can use light mayo if you prefer).

Preheat the oven to 350°F.

Heat 1½ tablespoons of the oil in a pan, and fry the onion for about 4 minutes until soft. Add the ginger and garlic, and cook for another 40 seconds. Stir in the ground coriander, red chili powder, salt, and garam masala, and cook for another 20 seconds, then take off the heat. Add the lemon juice, cilantro, crab, egg, and mayonnaise. Stir well and add the breadcrumbs. Divide into eight portions and form into patties.

Heat 1 tablespoon of oil in a pan, and cook the crab cakes in batches, depending how big your pan is, over a low–moderate heat, for about 2 minutes on each side until golden. Place them on a baking tray in the oven to keep warm while you cook the rest. Add the remaining oil when cooking the second batch of cakes.

To make the tamarind mayonnaise, simply whisk all the ingredients together, taste, and adjust seasoning. Serve the crab cakes with a spoonful of the mayo with salad leaves on the side.

Serves 2

2 halibut steaks or other firm white fish
2 heaped tablespoons shredded coconut
2 heaped tablespoons flour
1½ tablespoons vegetable oil
½ lemon, to serve

Marinade

¾–1 large fat red chili, seeded and
    roughly chopped
1¼ in. fresh ginger (see page 12),
    roughly chopped
3 large garlic cloves, peeled and roughly
    chopped
2 teaspoons white wine vinegar
2 teaspoons ground coriander
8 fenugreek seeds
salt, to taste
¼ teaspoon freshly ground black pepper
1 teaspoon vegetable oil

Coconut and Chili Pan-fried Halibut

This delicious recipe is my own version of the traditional Keralan way of frying fish. It works beautifully with any firm, white-fleshed fish, so find out what is fresh at your local fishmongers or supermarket fish counter. The dish isn't as spicy as it might first appear, for the cooking mellows the flavors and they form only a thin coating on the fish. Really easy to make and perfect for a summer's day, this fish goes well with the Chopped Salad with Coconut and Peanuts (see page 103), which is an evocative combination of the flavors of the same coastline.

Pound or blend together the marinade ingredients to make a fine purée. Over-season the mixture slightly, as it will be absorbed by the fish. Place the fish in the marinade in a nonmetallic bowl, and leave for at least 30 minutes.

Mix together the coconut and the flour. Maintaining a generous coating of the purée, coat both sides of the fish steaks well in the dry mixture.

Heat the oil in a large nonstick saucepan and, when hot, add the fish. Cook on a low heat without moving the fish for 4 minutes, then turn over and cook on the other side for another 3–4 minutes or until done. Squeeze some lemon juice over the fish, and serve hot with a salad.

1 tablespoon white poppy seeds
1 teaspoon mustard seeds
2 heaped tablespoons plain yogurt
¾ in. fresh ginger (see page 12), chopped
½–1 green chili, chopped
salt, to taste
good pinch of black pepper
1 teaspoon ground coriander
1 handful fresh cilantro stalks and leaves, chopped
2 pieces of white-fleshed fillets, such as haddock or flounder
vegetable oil
⅔ tablespoon butter
lemon juice, to taste

Bengali-style Baked Fish

Bengali food is quite unique and different from all other Indian regional cuisine. Here cooks use subtle flavors but are generous in their use of eye-watering mustard, both the oil and the seeds. They cherish their fresh seafood, and their cuisine is almost a homage to the slippery creatures. This Bengali-style recipe is a delicious example of their food, but I've simplified and mellowed it a little. I love this dish—it takes just minutes to prepare, the same to cook, and tastes wonderful. Serve with fresh vegetables or with the Warm Corn, Coconut, and Watercress salad on page 99.

Preheat the oven to 375°F.

Make a paste of the poppy seeds, mustard seeds, yogurt, ginger, and chili. I use a pestle and mortar, but you can use a blender instead. Stir in the salt, pepper, ground coriander, and cilantro. Taste and adjust the seasoning.

Place the fish in a well-oiled roasting pan. Coat the top of the fish with a good layer of the paste and dot with the butter. Cook for 7–10 minutes or until tender (it depends on the type of fish and the thickness). Drizzle with lemon juice and serve.

Serves 4–6

Dumplings

⅝ cup rice flour
½ teaspoon salt
⅜ cup warm water
scant ¼ cup creamed coconut, grated

Curry

1 teaspoon cumin seeds
2 teaspoons coriander seeds
9 black peppercorns
¾ teaspoon mustard seeds
¾ teaspoon turmeric powder
good pinch of carom seeds
1–2 teaspoons red chili powder, or
    to taste
5 large garlic cloves, peeled
1 large onion, peeled, one half roughly
    chopped and the other minced
⅝ cup creamed coconut, broken up
2½ cups water
2 tablespoons vegetable or coconut
    oil
1½–2 teaspoons tamarind paste
salt, to taste
14 oz. shrimp, shelled but with the tail
    left intact and cleaned

Mangalorean Shrimp Curry with Rice Dumplings

This is a delectable, vibrant curry from the southwest coast of India, a region dominated by fresh seafood, coconuts, bright red chilies, and a love of spices. This dish would usually be cooked only on special occasions, as the rice for the dumplings would require overnight soaking, drying during the day, and then grinding by hand, but we are fortunate to be able to buy ground rice. These dumplings have a subtle flavor and texture that go really well with the curry. You can, however, omit them and serve the curry with rice, if you wish.

For the dumplings, mix all the ingredients in a bowl until you have soft, pliable dough. Divide and roll into 12 balls or into any shape you like—I like to squeeze them in my palm to make some indentations, which catch pools of curry in them. Steam for 12 minutes and set aside.

Meanwhile, start the curry. Place all the spices, garlic, the roughly chopped onion, coconut, and one-third of the water in a blender, and blend until very smooth.

Heat the oil in a nonstick pan, and fry the remaining onion until light brown. Add the spice paste and cook over a medium heat until the water has dried up, then continue cooking the paste for 6–7 minutes, stirring regularly.

Add the remaining water, tamarind, and salt to taste, and bring to a boil. Cook over a moderate heat for 10 minutes. Taste and adjust the salt and tamarind paste. Add the shrimp and simmer over a low heat for 3–4 minutes. Add the dumplings and simmer for another minute or until the shrimp are cooked and the dumplings warmed through.

Serves 3–4

1 in. fresh ginger (see page 12)
4 large garlic cloves, peeled
1–5 dried, mild red chilies (depending
    on your tolerance and the quality of
    the chilies)
2 cloves
6 peppercorns
1 teaspoon cumin seeds
½ tablespoon brown mustard seeds
½ teaspoon turmeric
2½ tablespoons vegetable oil
1 small onion, peeled and finely chopped
2 medium tomatoes, finely chopped
1 green chili, left whole
3–4 tablespoons red wine vinegar, or
    to taste
1 teaspoon sugar
salt, to taste
¾ lb. small raw shrimp, shelled and
    cleaned

Shrimp Balchao

This Goan dish is spicy, tangy, and full of flavor. It is how those living on the southern coast take advantage of the fresh, seasonal, and cheap shrimp that come their way before the monsoons set in and their supply runs dry. They buy baskets of the small shrimp and use them to make this relish, which lasts them through the "dry" season and into the following year. A little goes a long way, as it is spicy but very tempting and is an accompaniment, rather than a main dish. If you want to use it as a relish and keep it for a while, fry the shrimp before adding them to the masala paste, so there is no more moisture left in them. The gravy is moist and clings to the shrimp as an envelope of flavor.

Make a paste of the ginger, garlic, red chilies, and all the spices, using a little water until you achieve a fine paste.

Heat the oil in a large nonstick saucepan, and fry the onion until golden brown. Add the tomatoes and green chili, and fry for about 10–12 minutes over a moderate to high heat until the mixture becomes a deep burgundy color. Add a splash of water whenever the pan runs dry.

Add the spice paste and fry for about 5 minutes until the oil leaves the masala. Add the vinegar, sugar, and a good amount of salt. Cook for another minute and taste for the balance of flavors. Adjust as you like.

Add the shrimp and cook for about 2 minutes until done. To keep as a relish, store in sterilized jars in the fridge.

Serves 4

16 large king shrimp, shelled but with the tail left intact, deveined and cleaned
4 wooden skewers, soaked in water for 30 minutes
1 tablespoon melted butter, for basting
½ lemon
1 teaspoon chaat masala
lettuce leaves, lime halves, sliced tomato, red onion, and green chutney, to serve

Marinade

¾ cup Greek-style yogurt, strained
2 tablespoons ground mustard seeds
1 teaspoon white wine vinegar
⅝ in. fresh ginger (see page 12)
3 large garlic cloves, peeled
pinch of turmeric
½ teaspoon red chili powder
2 tablespoons mustard oil or any mild oil
¼ teaspoon garam masala
salt, to taste

Tandoori Shrimp flavored with Mustard

These tandoori shrimp are succulent and indulgent, but manage to remain quite light and healthful. They are the perfect summer barbecue food for friends, but work just as well as an appetizer or a light meal with a salad. We serve these all year round with a little green chutney (see page 134) as a predinner appetizer with drinks, to whet the appetite and awaken the taste buds.

Purée the marinade ingredients together with a hand blender until smooth. Place the shrimp in the marinade in a nonmetallic bowl and leave for 30 minutes, if possible.

Preheat the oven to 400°F. Oil a baking sheet.

Slide the shrimp onto the skewers and place on the baking sheet. Bake in the oven for 4 minutes. Baste with butter and cook for another 1–2 minutes or until the shrimp are done.

Drizzle a little lemon juice over and sprinkle with the chaat masala. Serve on a bed of lettuce with some lime halves, sliced tomato, and red onion and with some green chutney on the side.

2 medium onions, peeled and cut
    into chunks
1 in. fresh ginger (see page 12) cut
    into chunks
4 cloves
6 green cardamom pods
2 large sticks of cinnamon
3 tablespoons vegetable oil
2 large garlic cloves, peeled and made
    into a paste
3–6 green chilies, slit lengthwise
    but left whole
¾ teaspoon turmeric
1 rounded teaspoon ground coriander
1½ –1¾ cups coconut milk
salt, to taste
1 teaspoon sugar, or to taste
1 lb. 5 oz. medium–large tiger shrimp,
    shelled but with the tail left intact,
    deveined and cleaned
⅓ cup coconut cream (optional)

Bengali Shrimp in a Mild Coconut Gravy

I love this dish. It has the heat and pungency of the green chilies, but the actual spices provide the background flavors and are quite mild. It is a hugely popular dish from Bengal, based on the beautiful local tiger shrimp. I use both coconut milk and cream, as this dish has a rich coconut flavor, which would normally be derived from grating and extracting thick and thin milks from fresh coconuts. However, for speed, I cheat and use store-bought versions. If you wish, you can add a little extra milk and omit the coconut cream altogether.

Blend the onions with the ginger to a fine paste. Grind together 2 cloves, 3 cardamom pods, and 1 cinnamon stick in a pestle and mortar; set aside.

Heat the oil in a large nonstick pan, add the remaining whole spices, and fry for 20 seconds or until fragrant. Add the onion paste and fry over a low heat, stirring frequently, for 8–10 minutes until golden brown. It is important that the onions be cooked through.

Add the garlic, chilies, turmeric, ground coriander, and a splash of water, and cook for 1 minute. Stir in the coconut milk, salt, and sugar, bring to a boil, then simmer over a low heat for 3–4 minutes. Add the shrimp and simmer for 2–3 minutes until cooked. Stir in the reserved ground spices and coconut cream, if using, and serve.

3 tablespoons vegetable oil
1 small onion, peeled and minced
2–4 green chilies, left whole
4 large garlic cloves, peeled and made
    into a paste
1¼ in. fresh ginger (see page 12), made
    into a paste
salt, to taste
3 tomatoes, chopped into large dice
2¼ lb. mussels, scrubbed under water
    and de-bearded; discard any that are
    already open
½ teaspoon turmeric
1 tablespoon garam masala
scant ½ cup shredded coconut
handful of fresh cilantro leaves and
    stalks, chopped

Mussels with Dry Coconut

This coastal dish, from the southwestern state of Maharashtra, is quick and easy to make and really delicious. I always consider mussels a summery ingredient, but only because I always ate them under the sun, by the sea, and on vacation. The flavors of this recipe are well rounded—the tartness from the tomatoes contrasts wonderfully with the sweetness provided by the coconut and mussels, while the various spices add a good background flavor. I serve this dish with some of the mussels in their shells and others taken out and stirred into the curry, making an appetizing and dramatic plate. The masala should be thick enough to coat the mussels and get into any shells.

Heat the oil in a medium nonstick pan and fry the onion until golden brown. Add the chilies, garlic and ginger pastes, and salt, and stir well for 20 seconds. Add the tomatoes and cook for about 8 minutes, until they have softened and start to break down.

Meanwhile, cook the mussels in a large pot of boiling water until they have opened, around 3 minutes. Remove them with a slotted spoon and set aside. Reserve the water. Discard any mussels that have not opened.

Add the turmeric, garam masala, and coconut to the onion mixture, and mix well. Then stir in the cooked mussels —some on and some off their shell works best. Add a good splash of the cooking water and stir through. Stir in the cilantro and serve with chapati, naan, or even a hunk of ordinary bread.

Southern Indian Mixed Vegetable Dish

Smashed-fried Potatoes

Five-seed
Potatoes

Stir-fried Green Onions

Spinach with Tomatoes

Chopped Salad with Coconut and Peanuts

Sweetcorn Curry

Okra

Fried Spiced

Herb and Peanut-dressed
Spinach Salad

Paneer with Spinach

VEGETABLES

Stuffed Jalapeño
Chilies in Yogurt

Warm Corn, Coconut, and Watercress

Stir-fried Nigella Cabbage

Bengali-style Eggplant
cooked in Yogurt

Serves 6

⅝ cup shredded coconut
2 ½ tablespoons vegetable oil
1 teaspoon cumin seeds
½ medium onion, peeled and sliced
1–2 green chilies, slit lengthwise but
   left whole
¼ teaspoon turmeric
salt, to taste
2 medium potatoes, peeled and cut
   into quarters lengthwise and then
   sliced crosswise on the diagonal
2 medium carrots, peeled and cut into
   fat batons

6-in. piece of cucumber, halved
   lengthwise, seeds scooped out and
   cut crosswise into ½-in. pieces
1 generous cup green beans, ends
   trimmed and sliced diagonally
   crosswise into three
3 large or 4 small shallots, peeled and
   halved
1½ in. fresh ginger (see page 12),
   roughly chopped
2 handfuls of frozen peas
12 curry leaves
5 level tablespoons plain yogurt (fresh,
   not sour)
1 tablespoon coconut oil (optional)

Southern Indian Mixed Vegetable Dish

Known as avial, this recipe is one of the most famous vegetable dishes from Tamil Nadu, one of India's southernmost states. And, as such, it has all the elements of the south with the exception of the choice of fresh vegetables—here, I've chosen less exotic ones to make your shopping easier. You can pair this recipe with any seasonal vegetables, although it really does need something starchy, such as the potatoes used here. The dish is often served at feasts, but I have reduced the amount of oil and coconut used and happily eat it for lunch with some rice or as part of a meal. It is a deceptively easy dish to make—all the work is in the preparation of the vegetables.

Soak the coconut in water to cover while you prepare the vegetables.

Heat the oil in a large nonstick pan. Add the cumin, onion, and chilies, and sauté for about 4–5 minutes until the onions are soft and coloring. Add the turmeric, salt, potatoes, and carrots, and cook for 14 minutes, covered, over a low heat. Stir frequently to make sure the vegetables don't catch on the base of the pan, adding a sprinkle of water if necessary. Add the cucumber and beans, and continue cooking in the same way until the vegetables are all tender, another 6–7 minutes or so.

Meanwhile, blend together the shallots, ginger, and coconut, along with its soaking water, to make a fine paste. Add to the pan with the peas, and cook, stirring often, for 5 minutes. Tear the curry leaves to release their aroma and add to the pan, give it a good stir, and add the yogurt. Turn off the heat and mix well, pouring the coconut oil over, if using.

vegetable oil, for frying
1 lb. 5 oz. medium-sized red-skinned
    potatoes, peeled and halved
    lengthwise
salt, to taste
1/2 teaspoon dried mango powder
1/4 – 1/2 teaspoon red chili powder
1/2 teaspoon ground coriander

Smashed-fried Potatoes

I very rarely deep-fry anything, as I think there are other, more healthful ways of enjoying the same ingredient. However, these unusual potatoes really are worth enjoying in this simple, if slightly wicked, way. They hail from the Sindhi community and are really quick and fun to make. They are a fantastic accompaniment to barbecues, burgers, and any outdoor meals. The dish works best with smallish, red-skinned potatoes, since they don't break up when pressed. Alternatively, you can fry some large potato wedges and toss them in the spices.

Heat vegetable oil to a depth of 3 in. in a wide saucepan or wok. Toss the potatoes with a little salt to season and add them to the oil. Fry over a low heat for about 15 minutes, turning occasionally, until they are soft in the center when tested with the point of a sharp knife. They will still be pale in color.

Remove from the oil with a slotted spoon, and leave to drain on a plate lined with paper towels for 5 minutes. Then, using your fingers, lightly flatten the potatoes.

To serve, reheat the oil in the pan, add the flattened potatoes and fry them over a low heat for about 5–6 minutes until they are golden and crisp. Remove and drain on paper towels once again, and sprinkle a little of each of the spices over the top. Check seasoning and add extra, if necessary. Top each potato with a drop or two of oil to set the powdery spices, and serve.

Serves 4–5

1 lb. 2 oz. small new potatoes
3 tablespoons vegetable oil
2 teaspoons panch phoran (also known
    as Bengali 5-Seed Blend)
$\frac{3}{4}$ teaspoon turmeric
salt, to taste
$\frac{1}{4}$ – $\frac{1}{2}$ teaspoon red chili powder or 1–2
    dried red chilies
handful of fresh cilantro leaves and
    stalks, chopped

Five-seed Potatoes

These simple and delicious potatoes require little more than a handful of ingredients yet are good enough to serve to your most distinguished friends. Panch phoran is a blend of equal quantities of cumin, fennel, mustard, nigella, and fenugreek seeds, and it provides a fantastic yet complex flavor and a nuttiness that goes beautifully with the potatoes. I use small new potatoes, because I think they look more natural and beautiful than cubes of potato, but there is no real difference when it comes to taste, so use whichever is easier for you.

Boil the potatoes until just soft, then cool slightly and peel.

Place the oil and seeds in a large saucepan, and heat gently so the oil can absorb the flavors of the seeds. Then allow them to fry over a low heat for 20 seconds and add the turmeric, salt, and chili powder or dried chilies. Give the pan a good stir, add the potatoes, and coat evenly in the spices. Cook over a low heat, stirring just occasionally, for 3–4 minutes.

Turn up the heat and do not stir the potatoes, allowing them to form a nice crust on their base, then stir and allow to brown on the other side. Once the potatoes have browned a little all over, take the pan off the heat and serve the potatoes garnished with the cilantro.

Serves 4

8 large, fat green chilies
1 medium–large potato, boiled, skin removed, and mashed
2 tablespoons vegetable oil, plus an extra 1 teaspoon
1 teaspoon mustard seeds
¾ teaspoon cumin seeds
½ teaspoon large fennel seeds
2–3 tablespoons water
2½ tablespoons shredded coconut
7 tablespoons yogurt
salt, to taste
15 curry leaves

Stuffing

¼ teaspoon turmeric
½ teaspoon ground cumin
½–1 teaspoon lemon juice, to taste
1 tablespoon chopped onion, softened in 2 teaspoons vegetable oil (optional)
salt, to taste

Stuffed Jalapeño Chilies in Yogurt

There are so many varieties of chilies in India, and indeed here on our doorstep, that it is often difficult to know which ones to use when and how hot they are once cooked. The general rule is that the smaller they are, the hotter they are. Many supermarkets now sell these large, fat green chilies, which are ideal for stuffing. If using jalapeños, try to find large ones, as the stuffing detracts from the heat, as does the yogurt. It might seem like a complicated dish, but it is really easy, just with many components.

Blanch the chilies in boiling salted water for 2 minutes, then drain on paper towels. Slit the chilies on the straightest side to make a pocket. Scoop out the seeds and membranes and discard.

Add the stuffing ingredients to the mashed potato and mix together well. Stuff the chilies with just enough mixture to fill.

Heat 2 tablespoons of the oil in a large skillet. Add ½ teaspoon each of the mustard and cumin seeds, and, when they pop, add the fennel seeds. Cook for another 20 seconds, then add the chilies. Sauté over a low heat until they have softened but not lost their shape, about 7–9 minutes.

Meanwhile, whisk the water and coconut into the yogurt, and season. Heat the remaining oil in a small pan and add the remaining mustard and cumin seeds and the curry leaves. Cook for 20–30 seconds and stir into the yogurt. Leave to cool while the chilies finish cooking.

To serve, place the chilies on a plate and pour the cool yogurt over them.

Serves 3–4

2–3 tablespoons vegetable oil
1 teaspoon cumin seeds
4 medium cooking tomatoes, puréed
1 rounded teaspoon ground coriander
½ teaspoon turmeric
¼ – ½ teaspoon red chili powder
¼ teaspoon garam masala
salt, to taste
4 generous cups baby spinach leaves

Spinach with Tomatoes

Spinach is a favorite vegetable in the West, as well as in India. I think the main reasons for this are that it is easy to find, quick to cook, and really good for you. Indians tend to overcook their spinach, thereby sacrificing a lot of its freshness and nutrition. Like many of my generation, I want to retain the goodness that comes with these leafy beauties, so I have created this simple, fresh, and delicious dish which really delivers both flavor and food values. This recipe can be made with less oil, if you wish, but the oil does round off the sharpness that can accompany spinach.

Heat the oil in a nonstick pan. Add the cumin seeds and fry for about 20 seconds, until aromatic. Add the puréed tomatoes, coriander, turmeric, chili powder, and garam masala, as well as salt to taste. Cook for about 6–7 minutes or until you can see oil bubbling on the sides of the tomatoes. Taste to check that the rawness of the tomatoes has gone. Add the spinach, stir, and cook for about 5–7 minutes, or until well wilted and most of the excess water has dried off, then serve.

Serves 2–3

1 tablespoon mustard or vegetable oil
small pinch of asafetida
½ teaspoon brown mustard seeds
½ teaspoon nigella seeds
1–2 small dried red chilies, left whole
1 teaspoon skinned, split black gram
    lentils (urad dal), washed
1 heaped tablespoon peanuts, chopped
10–15 curry leaves, torn in half
½ white cabbage, finely shredded
salt, to taste

Stir-fried Nigella Cabbage

I think this easy recipe is one the best ways to cook cabbage, and the dish can be eaten as a hot salad, a snack, or part of a meal. The strong, peppery flavors are enhanced by the mustard oil, although you can use good old vegetable oil if that's what you have on hand in the kitchen. If you prefer a milder dish, you can omit the chilies, although they do provide extra flavor. Raw peanuts are the best ones to use, but if you have only roasted ones, add them in toward the end of cooking, just to heat them through.

Heat the oil in a large wok or nonstick saucepan. Add the asafetida and the mustard and nigella seeds and fry for 30 seconds or until they pop. Add the chilies, lentils, and peanuts. Turn the heat down and fry until the lentils start to color, then add the curry leaves, cabbage, and salt to taste.

Stir-fry for 3 minutes, then cover the pan and cook on a low heat for another 6–7 minutes or until the cabbage has wilted but still retains some bite.

7 cups baby spinach leaves, washed
3 tablespoons vegetable oil
1 teaspoon cumin seeds
1 large onion, peeled and chopped
2 in. fresh ginger (see page 12), sliced
    into long julienne strips
1½ tablespoons chopped garlic
1–2 green chilies, left whole
2 teaspoons ground coriander
salt, to taste
4 cups milk, made into around 9 oz.
    paneer with fresh yogurt (see
    page 26)
½ –1 teaspoon garam masala,
    depending on quality
⅜ cup whole milk or 4 tablespoons
    heavy cream
1–2 teaspoons lemon juice, or to taste

Paneer with Spinach

This is a wonderful velvety dish with large, fresh cubes of paneer. I don't add much chili, since the green ones are used more for flavor than for heat—I like this dish quite mild and creamy. The only spices are cumin, coriander, and garam masala, and that is just enough for a good background flavor and aroma. I use the cream when I have friends over, but the milk when it is just the family. It is probably an Indian thing of serving your guests the best ingredients, even if it's not the healthiest option—I leave it to you. Delicious with simple pilaff or naan.

Blanch the spinach leaves in hot water for 3 minutes or until well wilted. Drain into a colander and run under cold water until they cool. Blend to a smooth paste and set aside.

Heat the oil in a large nonstick pan. Add the cumin seeds and fry for about 30 seconds until fragrant. Add the onion and fry over a mild heat for about 6 minutes or until soft. Add the ginger, garlic, and chilies, and cook for 1 minute. Add the ground coriander and salt to taste. Cook for another 30 seconds, then add the spinach and a splash of water, if necessary. The mixture should be loose but not watery. Bring to a boil and simmer for 3 minutes.

Add the paneer cubes, garam masala, and milk or cream. Stir and cook for a few minutes or until the spinach is creamy. Before serving, stir in the lemon juice to taste.

Stir-fried Green Onions

Serves 4

1 tablespoon vegetable oil
½ teaspoon cumin seeds
½ teaspoon turmeric
1 teaspoon ground coriander
pinch of red chili powder
bunch of green onions, preferably
    thin ones, washed and sliced into
    small rounds, around ¼ in. long
salt, to taste

This is the quickest side dish you can make. It makes a punchy accompaniment to any dish, even plain layered breads. It is not a full vegetable dish but adds a burst of flavor, color, and texture to anything within minutes.

Heat the oil in a small nonstick saucepan. Add the cumin seeds and fry until lightly colored and fragrant. Add the rest of the spices, stir-fry for just 5–10 seconds, then add the green onions. Turn the heat up and stir-fry for 1 minute—they should still remain crunchy. Taste and adjust the seasoning and serve right away.

Sweetcorn Curry

Serves 6–8

1 medium onion, peeled and cut into
    large pieces
3 small cooking tomatoes, quartered
2 in. fresh ginger (see page 12), roughly
    chopped
3 large garlic cloves, peeled and halved
4 tablespoons vegetable oil
1 teaspoon cumin seeds
¾ teaspoon turmeric
½ –1 teaspoon chili powder, or to taste
2 teaspoons ground coriander
salt, to taste
5 cups frozen corn, defrosted
2 cups milk
2 tablespoons tomato paste
4 tablespoons plain yogurt
½ teaspoon garam masala

This pantry dish originates from my husband's family in Rajasthan, a desert state that relies on frozen, rather than fresh, vegetables.

Blend together the onion, tomatoes, ginger, and garlic to a fine paste.

Heat the oil in a large nonstick pan, and fry the cumin seeds for 30 seconds or until aromatic. Add the paste and cook, stirring often, over a moderate–high heat for 10 minutes or until the oil bubbles on the side of the pan.

Add the turmeric, chili, coriander, and salt, and stir for 1 minute. Add the corn and cook for 5 minutes. Add the milk and tomato paste, bring to a boil, and simmer for 15 minutes or until the curry no longer looks watery. Stir in the yogurt and garam masala, and serve.

Warm Corn, Coconut, and Watercress

Serves 3–4

1 tablespoon butter
1 teaspoon vegetable oil
1 teaspoon mustard seeds
12 curry leaves
1 teaspoon chopped ginger
1–2 small dry red chilies (optional)
2½ cups frozen or canned corn,
    drained and washed
1 cup milk
salt, to taste
2 tablespoons flaked coconut (or
    shredded if you don't have flaked)
handful of watercress, washed
1 teaspoon lemon juice, or to taste

This is a warm dish, which is almost a salad. The sweetness of the corn, texture of the coconut, warm spices, and piquant watercress taste sensational. Watercress is fairly rare in India, but we have our share of peppery leaves, which we often add to our salads.

Heat the butter and oil in a small, nonstick saucepan, and add the mustard seeds. Cook for a few seconds, covering the pan once they start to pop. Add the curry leaves, ginger, and chilies, and give the pan a good stir. Add the corn and milk; cook over a moderate heat for 12–15 minutes until there is little moisture left in the pan.

To serve, season and stir in the coconut, watercress, and lemon juice to taste.

14 oz. okra, wiped clean with damp
    paper towels, ends trimmed
4 tablespoons chickpea flour
vegetable oil, for frying
1 teaspoon chaat masala
¼ teaspoon salt
¼ teaspoon red chili powder
¼ teaspoon dried mango powder

Fried Spiced Okra

These crisp, fried strips of okra are so much better in the flesh than they might appear on paper. Whenever I have made this dish, there have never, ever been any leftovers. The chickpea flour on the okra helps them to crisp up beautifully, and the spices add all the flavor they need. Chaat masala is a blend of spices (see page 156) and is the key flavoring in this dish; but if you don't have any and prefer a simpler dish, give the recipe a try anyway, as this is the best way to cook okra. They need to be cooked when you want to eat them, as they do not reheat well.

Slice the okra lengthwise into quarters. If they are quite large, slice them again. Toss with the chickpea flour.

Heat the oil to a moderate–high heat in a large saucepan. Add all or half the okra, depending on the size of your pan. Fry for about 8 minutes, stirring occasionally, until the okra becomes crisp, with some just turning a rich golden brown color.

Turn the okra onto a plate lined with paper towels to drain, then tip into a bowl with the chaat masala, salt, chili, and dried mango powder, and toss well together. Serve hot.

3 handfuls of baby spinach leaves
½ shallot, peeled and sliced
1 tomato, sliced into thin wedges

Dressing

2 heaped tablespoons roasted peanuts
1 large handful fresh cilantro, leaves
    and stalks
1 small handful fresh mint leaves
salt, to taste
¼ teaspoon cumin
⅛ teaspoon garlic paste
⅛ teaspoon ginger paste
2–3 teaspoons lemon juice, or to taste
3–4 tablespoons vegetable oil, such as
    peanut oil

Herb and Peanut-dressed Spinach Salad

I love salads; and although in India we use different salad ingredients and don't often make a dressing, salads are always present on a well-set Indian table to provide extra crunch to a meal. They are generally dressed with a squeeze of lemon juice and a light sprinkling of salt and chili powder. This spinach salad is slightly different and is great with any meal, but it's really designed to be served alongside tandoori dishes.

Blend together all the ingredients for the dressing until well mixed. Lightly toss the spinach leaves, sliced shallot, and tomato in the dressing and serve.

Serves 2–4

1 tomato, minced
4 tablespoons minced cucumber
1 green chili, minced (optional)
2 tablespoons minced onion
1 handful of fresh cilantro leaves and
    stalks, chopped
salt, to taste
2 heaped tablespoons shredded coconut
3 tablespoons salted peanuts, roughly
    chopped
¼ teaspoon ginger paste
1 teaspoon vegetable oil
¼ teaspoon mustard seeds
1 sprig of curry plant, leaves only
1 tablespoon lemon juice, or to taste

Chopped Salad with Coconut and Peanuts

This simple salad is ideal served with a South Indian meal or as an accompaniment to any chicken or fish dish. It is a perfect summer salad, with different textures and clean, subtle flavors. I love raw onions, but if you find them a hard to digest, leave them out and add more cucumber instead. In typical Indian style, I prefer not to add a proper dressing but simply flavor the salad with mustard seeds and curry leaves.

Mix together the tomato, cucumber, green chili, onion, cilantro, salt, coconut, peanuts, and ginger paste.

Heat the oil in a small saucepan. Add the mustard seeds, and once they splutter, add the curry leaves and remove from the heat. Add the lemon juice and stir into the salad. Taste and adjust the seasoning.

Serves 4–5

14 oz. eggplants, thinly sliced into
    rounds
good pinch of turmeric
salt, to taste
¼ teaspoon red chili powder
2 tablespoons vegetable oil
1 generous cup plain yogurt
1–1½ teaspoons sugar
1 rounded teaspoon cumin seeds,
    roasted and ground
large handful of fresh cilantro leaves
    and stalks, chopped

Bengali-style Eggplant cooked in Yogurt

The first time I tried Bengali food was in a small, family-run restaurant that is a local treasure. In among an elaborate introduction to the region's food was this simple, modest accompaniment. I loved it immediately—it is a mild and creamy but confident and versatile dish. I have since tasted many variations, but when I make it at home I always end up recreating those original flavors. Eggplant is such an underused vegetable, but so delicious, and it goes well with lamb, chicken, fish, lentils, and most vegetables. This dish is perfect with Indian breads or even with fresh French bread.

Coat the eggplants in the turmeric, salt, and half the red chili powder, and fry in the oil in a large, nonstick skillet until soft and when the point of a knife goes through with no resistance. You may have to do this in two batches. Drain on a plate lined with paper towels and set aside.

Beat three-quarters of the yogurt with the sugar, salt to taste, and the remaining red chili powder, and add to a small saucepan. Heat, stirring, over a low heat until warm—this takes a good 5 minutes. Stir in the ground cumin seeds and the eggplants and cilantro. Cook for another minute. Turn off the heat and stir in the remaining yogurt. Check the seasoning and serve.

Toasted

Spiced Chickpeas

Slightly Sweet Bengal

Gram Lentil Curry

Fava Beans Thoran

Buttery Black Lentils

LENTILS
and
BEANS

Garlic and Chili
Split Pigeon Pea Curry

Simple Spinach
and Lentil Curry

1 generous cup whole black lentils,
    picked through, washed, and soaked
    for at least 3 hours
4 cups water
3 large garlic cloves, peeled
2 in. fresh ginger (see page 12), halved
    lengthwise
scant ¾ cup tomato paste
½–1 teaspoon red chili powder
2 green chilies, left whole
salt, to taste
2 tablespoons butter
½ onion, peeled and chopped
scant ¼ cup light cream
1 teaspoon garam masala
handful of fresh cilantro, to garnish

Buttery Black Lentils

For an Indian, this dish is king of the lentil curries, and it is perhaps the most popular lentil dish in any Indian restaurant. Known as makhni dal, it is a rich, creamy, and flavorful curry, which everyone seems to love. These lentils take a long time to cook and can be quite heavy to digest, so this is a dish we eat sparingly and on special occasions, which adds to its enjoyment. The lentils would traditionally be cooked overnight over the barest flame, so that they cook evenly and perfectly, but they are worth the wait. They are perfect with naan and raita, and not much else is needed.

Drain the lentils, discarding their soaking water, and put in a large saucepan with the fresh water. Bring to a boil and then simmer, covered, for about 1 hour or until tender.

Meanwhile, make a paste of the garlic and half the ginger. Finely slice the remaining ginger into long, fine shreds.

When the lentils are tender, add the tomato paste, chili powder, green chilies, salt, and the garlic-ginger paste to the pan. Stir well and cook for another 30 minutes. Keep an eye on the pan and give it an occasional stir, as the lentils have a tendency to settle on the base.

Heat the butter in a pan over a low heat, add the onion and sliced ginger, and cook for about 4–5 minutes until colored. Stir into the lentils along with the cream and garam masala. Cook for another minute and serve garnished with fresh cilantro.

2 tablespoons vegetable oil
1 teaspoon cumin seeds
½ teaspoon turmeric
¼ – ¾ teaspoon red chili powder
1¼ tablespoons ground coriander
1 teaspoon dried mango powder
¾ teaspoon garam masala
2½ cups canned chickpeas, drained
    and rinsed
salt, to taste
2 tablespoons boiled water
handful of fresh cilantro, chopped

Toasted Spiced Chickpeas

This dish is almost instantaneous yet manages to taste great and be healthful. The chickpeas are full of minerals and good fiber and always get a welcome. Ideally, you would eat this dish with Indian layered bread (parathas), but it also works well with naan or even toast. It is great stuffed generously into a warmed pita with a little dressed salad and green chutney (see page 134). It is also a good dish to have in your repertoire, because it can be thrown together when you have a vegetarian coming over for dinner and have to make an extra dish in a hurry.

Heat the oil in a nonstick saucepan. Add the cumin seeds and fry for about 30–40 seconds or until they give off their aroma and start to darken. Add the remaining spices and salt, and cook for 10 seconds. Add the chickpeas and stir to coat well in the spices. Cook for 2 minutes, then add the water and the cilantro leaves. Cook for another minute and serve.

1 generous cup yellow mung lentils
  (from skinned and split mung beans)
4 cups water
1 in. fresh ginger (see page 12), cut
  into thin strips
3 green chilies, left whole (optional)
¾ teaspoon turmeric
2 small tomatoes, puréed
2 scant cups baby spinach leaves
salt, to taste
1½ tablespoons ghee, butter, or
  vegetable oil
1 teaspoon cumin seeds
2 garlic cloves, peeled and cut into five
  large pieces
1 rounded teaspoon ground coriander
½ teaspoon garam masala

Simple Spinach and Lentil Curry

This dish is so simple to make and is typical of home fare. It is the kind of dish that a mother makes for her family, is good for all ages, and, despite the chilies, is not really too spicy. Now a confession—it could be better. I could add some whole spices and fry an onion with the other tempering ingredients, but generally, when at home, I would prefer to make something simple and healthful that tastes good rather than compete with heavier, restaurant fare. This curry is great with simple boiled rice, roti, or even toast.

Place the lentils, water, ginger, chilies, and turmeric in a pan, bring to a boil, then simmer over a moderate heat for 10 minutes. Stir in the tomatoes and cook for 20 minutes, then add the spinach and salt. Cook for another 10 minutes or so, until the lentils have started to break down and the curry comes together.

Meanwhile, heat the ghee, butter, or oil in a small pan. Add the cumin seeds and garlic and allow the cumin seeds to redden and the garlic to start to brown. Stir in the ground coriander and garam masala, then pour the mixture into the pan of lentils. Cook for another minute and serve.

1 tablespoon coconut or vegetable oil
½ teaspoon brown mustard seeds
½ teaspoon cumin seeds
½ small onion, peeled and finely chopped
1 teaspoon chopped fresh ginger
1 green chili, left whole
1½ cups fresh or frozen fava beans,
    thawed if using frozen
salt, to taste
½ cup grated fresh coconut
8 fresh curry leaves, torn in half

Fava Beans Thoran

I love tender, young, glistening fava beans just as they are and generally prefer not to cook them, but they are perfect in this simple South Indian dish. I feel the need to grate fresh coconut to go with these beans to retain their inherent freshness, and there is a simple, inexpensive gadget called a coconut scraper (see page 10) that helps me do this in minutes. If you are a coconut fan, it is well worth investing in one for beautiful, fluffy, sweet coconut flesh. This is a great side dish to accompany any summery meal or to eat as a quick protein snack.

Heat the oil in a pan, add the seeds, and fry for 30 seconds. Add the onion, ginger, and green chili, and cook for about 4 minutes over a lowish heat until the onions have softened.

Add the beans, salt, and a splash of water, and cook for 1 minute to warm through. Stir in the coconut and torn curry leaves, turn the heat down, cover, and cook for 2 minutes. Give the pan a stir and serve.

Serves 2–3

2 cups water
generous ¾ cup split pigeon pea lentils
    (toovar dal), picked over and
    washed
½ teaspoon turmeric
1 tablespoon ghee or vegetable oil
2–4 small dried red chilies, whole
    (I use bird's eye chilies)
1 rounded tablespoon chopped garlic
1 level tablespoon dried mango powder,
    or to taste
salt, to taste
1 tablespoon lemon juice, or to taste

Garlic and Chili Split Pigeon Pea Curry

This simple dish uses lots of pantry ingredients. It is the lentil equivalent of Italy's arabiatta ("angry") dishes—spicy, garlicky, and tart—using flavors that go really well with the savory lentils. Leaving the chilies whole adds flavor without the heat. These lentils break down into a purée, and as the dish cools it tends to firm up, so make sure the curry is not too thick before you take it off the heat.

Place the water and lentils in a saucepan and bring to a boil. Add the turmeric, cover, and simmer over a low heat for about 20 minutes or until tender. Uncover and cook over a moderate heat for about 10 minutes until the lentils completely break down. If the lentils are too watery, increase the heat.

Heat the ghee or oil in a separate, small, nonstick saucepan. Add the chilies and cook for a minute, then add the garlic. Cook over a moderate heat until the garlic is golden but not burned, then pour straight into the pan of lentils. Add the dried mango powder, salt, and lemon juice to taste—the quantities of these depend on how tart your dried mango powder is. Serve hot. This curry solidifies as it cools, so add extra water if you are going to leave it to reheat later.

Serves 4–6

1¾ cups Bengal gram, well washed
2 bay leaves
5 cups water
½ teaspoon turmeric
1 heaped teaspoon ground coriander
1 teaspoon garam masala
salt, to taste
2–3 teaspoon sugar
2 tablespoons mustard oil, unsalted
    butter, or ghee
5 green cardamom pods
1 teaspoon cumin seeds
5 cloves
2-in. stick of cinnamon
½ teaspoon brown mustard seeds
1–2 dried red chilies
3 heaped tablespoons flaked or
    shredded coconut, or ¼ small fresh
    coconut, flesh cut into small dice

Slightly Sweet Bengal Gram Lentil Curry

This popular Bengali dish is simple food and subtly spiced, as is most Bengali food. The lentils are meant to be thick, sweet, and savory, and they usually have raisins and coconut slivers to garnish; but I've omitted the raisins, simply because I'm not fond of fruit in curries. It is usually made with fresh coconut, but here I have changed it to dried, just because it is easier. It is normally eaten with the traditional luchi, a delicious deep-fried bread, but when I can't face the heaviness, naan, or even a simple rice dish, also goes really well with it.

Place the lentils, bay leaves, water, and turmeric in a pan, bring to a boil, and then simmer, covered, for around 50–60 minutes or until soft. Add extra water, if necessary.

Stir in the coriander and garam masala, salt, and sugar to taste. Cook until the lentils are completely soft and start to break up—I have an Indian wooden whisk that is ideal for this, but try anything that helps to break them up a little. You should be left with a thick lentily mass but with the actual lentils still discernible.

To serve, heat the oil or butter in a small pan (if using mustard oil, heat until smoking, then cool and reheat), and fry the cardamom pods, cumin, cloves, cinnamon, mustard seeds, and chilies for 30 seconds. Add the coconut and cook until it turns golden, then pour the mixture over the lentils. Stir in or leave to stir at the table.

Basmati Rice

Simple Pilaff

Spinach Pilaff

Lemon Rice

Wild Mushroom Pilaff

Creamy Rice and Lentils

BREAD
and
RICE

Coconut Rice

Simple
Layered
Flat
Breads

Roti

Naan

Basmati Rice

Serves 4

1 cup Basmati rice, cleaned in several washes of water until the water runs clear
1½ cups water
½ teaspoon lemon juice (optional)

Perfect Basmati rice is fluffy and delicate. It has a wonderful fragrance that is reminiscent of an Indian meal, but in reality many southern regions use their own indigenous rice, which is thicker, shorter, and nuttier. The basic rule is one part rice to one and a half parts water, but the longer you soak it the less water it needs—the moisture from the soaked rice can amount to more than you think.

Soak the rice in fresh, cold water for 30 minutes for long and fluffy grains.

Drain and tip into a thick-bottomed pan for even cooking. Add the water and bring to a good boil. Add the lemon juice, if using, and give it a good stir. Cover tightly, turn the heat right down, and cook for 7–8 minutes. Check after 7 minutes —the grains should be cooked, but if not, cover and test again after another minute.

Turn off the heat and uncover. Allow any excess moisture to evaporate from the pan for 5 minutes, then fluff up with a fork and serve.

Spinach Pilaff

Serves 3–4

2 tablespoons oil
1 bay leaf
2 black cardamom pods
6 black peppercorns
1 teaspoon cumin seeds
1–2 green chilies, forked but left whole
1 small onion, peeled and chopped
2 cups cooked Basmati rice (see recipe on the left for method)
2 scant cups baby spinach leaves, wilted in a pan and puréed
salt, to taste
2–3 teaspoons lemon juice, or to taste

This pilaff works well as part of any North Indian meal, but also makes a good partner for broiled chicken, simple lamb dishes, or chops, or even an assortment of broiled vegetables. The spices give it a wonderful rounded flavor, and the spinach provides a velvety texture. The fact that it is really good for us is a bonus. It is, needless to say, great for children—my young daughter loves it (even with the chili) and I haven't yet needed to hide the greenery!

Heat the oil in a large saucepan, add the whole spices and green chilies, and cook for 20 seconds. Add the onion and cook for about 4 minutes until translucent. Stir in the rice, spinach, and salt, and stir-fry to heat through. Just before serving, add lemon juice to taste.

Lemon Rice

Serves 2–3

2 tablespoons vegetable oil
½ teaspoon mustard seeds
pinch of fenugreek seeds
¾ teaspoon split Bengal gram
¾ teaspoon split black gram (Beluga lentils)
3 heaped tablespoons peanuts, coarsely chopped (raw is best)
1–2 dried red chilies, left whole
1 teaspoon chopped ginger
¼ teaspoon turmeric
10 curry leaves, torn in half
salt, to taste
3 tablespoons lemon juice, or to taste
2 cups cooked Basmati rice (see left)

This is a simple, fragrant rice and makes the perfect partner to any South Indian coconut dishes, as the tang of the lemon contrasts beautifully with the rich, sweet coconut. This vibrant dish would be wonderful with any of the fish, chicken, or lamb dishes in this book.

Heat the oil in a large nonstick skillet and add both seeds, the lentils, raw peanuts (if using), and chilies, and stir-fry until the lentils are light brown. Add the ginger, turmeric, curry leaves, and salt, and cook for 40 seconds.

Add the lemon juice and cook for another minute. Add the rice and roasted peanuts (if using instead of raw peanuts). Stir-fry to heat through, being careful not to break up the grains too much. Serve hot.

Opposite: *Basmati Rice, left; Spinach Pilaff, top right; Lemon Rice, bottom right.*

Coconut Rice

Serves 2

2 tablespoons vegetable oil
½ teaspoon mustard seeds
½ teaspoon cumin seeds
2 dried red chilies, whole
1 teaspoon split Bengal gram
1 teaspoon split black gram
½ small onion, peeled and chopped
1 teaspoon minced ginger
salt and freshly ground black pepper, to taste
2–3 tablespoons roasted cashew nuts, broken up
10 curry leaves
1½ cups cooked Basmati rice (see page 120)
4 tablespoons shredded coconut; soak in water to cover before you cook (it will absorb most of the water)

This rice is from Andra Pradesh, a southern region known for its seafood and red chilies, and this subtly-flavored recipe is a perfect foil for such ingredients. Fresh coconut has the best flavor, but you can use shredded.

Heat the oil in a large nonstick skillet, add the mustard seeds, cumin seeds, chilies, and both lentils, and fry until the latter start to color. Add the onion and ginger, and cook over a moderate heat for 4 minutes or until the onion is soft.

Add salt, pepper, cashews, curry leaves, rice, and soaked coconut and stir-fry over a moderate heat until the rice is hot and all the flavors combined. Check the seasoning and serve.

Opposite: *Coconut Rice*

Creamy Rice and Lentils

Serves 1

generous ⅛ cup Basmati rice
¼ cup split and husked yellow mung lentils
1 rounded teaspoon ghee
½ teaspoon cumin seeds
½ small onion, peeled and chopped
1 green chili, left whole (optional)
½ teaspoon chopped fresh ginger
½ garlic clove, peeled and chopped
salt, to taste
½ teaspoon turmeric
1¾ cups water
¼ teaspoon garam masala
¼ teaspoon freshly ground black pepper

This dish is easy to digest, nutritious and the first "real" food babies eat. Eat with plain yogurt and perhaps a relish.

Wash the rice in water, then soak the rice and lentils in water for 30 minutes.

Heat the ghee in a medium–large nonstick saucepan. Add the cumin and fry for 20 seconds until coloring and aromatic. Add the onion and sauté for 4 minutes until soft. Add the chili, ginger, garlic, and salt, and cook for 30 seconds, then add the drained rice and lentils, turmeric, and water.

Bring to a boil for a few minutes, then simmer for 30 minutes until the rice and lentils are tender and breaking down to form a mass. Stir in the garam masala and pepper and adjust the seasoning.

The dish thickens as it cools, so you may need to add a little water if you reheat.

Simple Pilaff

Serves 4

2 tablespoons vegetable oil
1 teaspoon cumin seeds
1 small onion, peeled and thinly sliced
1 teaspoon garam masala
salt, to taste
1 cup Basmati or long-grain white rice, washed and soaked for 30 minutes
¾ cup frozen peas
1½ cups water
1–2 tablespoons lemon juice, or to taste

This is a quick and easy pilaff. Usually I add whole spices, as it is, at heart, a spiced rice dish, but I realized it is better to encourage people to cook my food with a little compromise, rather than not at all. So here is the result—a simple pilaff made with powdered spices.

Heat the oil in a large nonstick saucepan. Add the cumin seeds and cook for about 30 seconds until fragrant. Add the onion and sauté for about 6 minutes until lightly caramelized. Add the garam masala and salt, and cook, stirring, for another 20 seconds.

Stir in the drained rice and frozen peas, then add the water. Taste for seasoning. Bring to a boil, then cook, covered, on the lowest heat for 10 minutes. Check that the grains are tender; if not, leave to steam for another 2 minutes. Then remove the lid and allow any moisture to evaporate. Drizzle the lemon juice over and gently mix in with a fork, fluffing up the grains.

Serves 4–6

1½ cups Basmati rice
½ lb. good-quality wild mushrooms such
    as girolles, morels, ceps, oyster, etc.
3 tablespoons vegetable oil
1 small onion, peeled and chopped into
    ½-in. dice
large handful of raw cashew nuts, whole
2 garlic cloves, peeled and minced
salt, to taste
1¾ cups water
1 teaspoon lemon juice, or to taste

Whole spices

1 teaspoon cumin seeds
2 bay leaves
1 large stick of cinnamon
2 black cardamom pods
6 green cardamom pods
6 black peppercorns
4 cloves

Wild Mushroom Pilaff

This is a special-occasion, statement pilaff. It is a dish cooked either for those you love or for those you really want to love you. It is a dish that may send you on a treasure hunt for delicious wild mushrooms that will cost a little more than your standard button ones, but the results are well worth the extra effort. The delicate flavors of mushrooms and Basmati rice marry beautifully. The onion and cashew nuts add a hint of sweetness and texture to make the dish a sublime but subtle experience. Whole spices add a wonderfully rounded flavor, but if you don't have any, leave them out and simply add one rounded teaspoon of garam masala instead (stir in with the mushrooms).

Wash the rice well and soak in cold water while you prepare the mushrooms. If using dried mushrooms, soak in just-boiled water for 20 minutes, then drain. Wash the morels well and wipe the other mushrooms clean with damp paper towels. Cut any large mushrooms into slices.

Heat the oil in a large, wide saucepan. Add the whole spices and cook for 20 seconds, then add the onion and cashew nuts. Fry for about 4–5 minutes until the onions are soft and browning at the edges. Add the mushrooms, garlic, and salt, and sauté over a high heat for 4–5 minutes.

Drain the rice and add to the pan of mushrooms with the water, bring to a good boil, then cover with a lid, lower the heat, and cook for 10 minutes. Taste a grain of rice to check if it's cooked; if not, leave for another minute. Take off the heat, remove the lid, and allow any excess moisture to evaporate. Gently stir in the lemon juice, and taste and adjust the seasoning, if necessary.

Makes 6

1 generous cup chapati flour, (or substitute half wholewheat and half all-purpose flour), plus extra for sprinkling
$\frac{1}{2}$ teaspoon salt
$\frac{3}{8}$–$\frac{1}{2}$ cup milk or water
3 tablespoons ghee or melted butter
1 teaspoon carom seeds

Simple Layered Flat Breads

These flat breads are so delicious, and you can serve them with any North Indian meal. They are usually eaten with vegetarian food, such as lentil curries, simple vegetable dishes, or scrambled eggs. When the breads are flavored with dried mint, sesame seeds, poppy seeds, carom seeds, or green onions, they are often eaten with plain yogurt and a relish.

Mix together the flour and salt in a large bowl. Add the milk or water slowly until you have a soft, non-sticky dough (it might not require all the liquid). Knead for about 8–10 minutes, until the mixture has formed a smooth dough. Cover with a damp dish towel and leave to rest for at least 10 minutes.

Divide the dough into six equal balls. Dust the balls lightly with flour. Take one and roll into a 6-in. circle. Using the back of a spoon or your fingers, smear ¾ teaspoon of ghee or melted butter over the surface; sprinkle a little flour over it and a pinch of carom seeds.

Roll the bread up as you would for a tight jelly roll, elongating the rope as you do by pulling the sides, for a long roll. Take one end of each piece of dough and coil it around on itself like rope. Press down with your fingers to flatten again. Dust with flour and roll out into a 5-in. circle.

Heat a nonstick skillet over a low heat. Place the dough onto the pan and turn the heat up a little. Once the top surface of the dough starts to dry out, turn it over. Take another ¾ teaspoon of ghee or butter, and spread it over the surface. For a flaky finish, slash all over with the edge of the spoon you are using.

Once the underside has become golden, turn again, and repeat with the ghee or butter and the spoon, and cook until golden. Place on a plate covered with paper towels, cover the bread with more paper, and keep warm while you make the rest.

1 generous cup chapati flour (or half
    wholewheat and half all-purpose
    flour)
salt (optional)
$3/8$–$1/2$ cup water

Roti

Roti (or chapati) is a basic wholewheat flat bread, which is eaten with almost every meal in northern India. These breads are soft, puff up when cooked, and, if you use a gas stove, lightly crisp on the underside. It is the easiest dough to make and doesn't require a bread machine. There is no real skill needed, and when it comes to rolling the dough into a circle, the old adage applies: practice makes perfect. You can find chapati flour in some supermarkets, but you could instead use equal quantities of wholewheat and all-purpose flour.

Sift the flour and salt, if using, into a bowl, and make a well in the center. Slowly drizzle in most of the water, and, using your hand, draw the flour into the center, mixing all the time. You may not need all the water, as flour absorbs different amounts of water, depending on its age and the moisture content in the air. It should be just slightly sticky.

Knead for 8–10 minutes. Then place in a bowl, cover with a damp dish towel, and leave for 30 minutes in a slightly warm area.

Divide the dough into six equal portions, and roll into golf-ball-sized rounds; cover. Flour your work surface and rolling pin. Roll each ball into thin circles with a diameter of 5–6 in. The best way of doing this is to keep rolling in one direction, turning the dough a quarter of a circle each time to get a round shape.

Heat a nonstick skillet until quite hot. Toss the roti from one hand to the other to remove any excess flour, and place in the pan. Turn the heat down to moderate, and cook until small bubbles appear on the underside, about 20–30 seconds, then turn. Cook this side until the base has small, dark beige spots.

The best way to puff up a cooked roti is to place it directly over an open flame (such as on a gas burner) using tongs. It will puff immediately, but leave for 3–5 seconds until dark spots appear, then turn and leave this side for a few seconds, and place on a plate. Repeat with the rest. If you have an electric burner, press down gently on the cooked roti—as you press one area, the rest should puff up. Then tackle the next area—the roti should puff up all over.

Keep the bread warm by wrapping in a napkin or foil and placing in a low oven while you make the rest. You can reheat the roti, wrapped, in a medium oven.

Makes 5

1¾ cups all-purpose flour
2 teaspoons sugar
½ teaspoon salt
½ teaspoon baking powder
½ cup (or a little extra) milk
2 tablespoons vegetable oil
nigella seeds, poppy seeds, sesame
    seeds, chopped garlic and fresh
    cilantro, or a mixture of pumpkin
    and sunflower seeds
1 tablespoon butter, melted, for
    brushing

Naan

Everyone loves naan. It is the quintessential restaurant bread, made with white rather than wholewheat flour, and is softer and more doughy than the other Indian flat breads. It is easy to make, and the real thing is quite different from the supermarket version, which also tastes great but always seems to be a cross-breed between the original and ordinary good bread. Naan should be soft, with a few crisp raised bits. Add a topping of your choice. I love nigella seeds the most, but even simple cilantro and garlic make a great topping.

Sift together the flour, sugar, salt, and baking powder. Mix together the milk and oil. Make a well in the center of the dry ingredients, and pour in the liquids.

Slowly mix together the dough by working outward from the center and incorporating the flour from the edges of the well to make a smooth, soft dough. Knead well for 8–10 minutes, adding a little flour if the dough is too sticky.

Place in an oiled bowl, cover with a damp dish towel, and leave for at least 1 hour in a warm place to rise. When risen, punch out and form into five balls.

Preheat the broiler to its highest setting and put a heavy baking sheet on the upper shelf.

Meanwhile, start to roll out the dough into teardrop or oval shapes, then gently prick all over with a fork. Sprinkle the seed topping over and press into the dough. Place the naans on the hot baking sheet and broil for 1–2 minutes or until there are brown spots on the surface. Brush with butter and serve hot.

Peshwari naan: to make this filled naan, pulse together ⅝ cup shelled pistachios, ¼ cup raisins and 1½ teaspoons fine granulated sugar to make a coarse powder. Divide into five portions. Roll the naan into thick circles, fill each with one portion of the filling and pinch the dough around it to close. Roll out the naan again into teardrop or oval shapes. Sprinkle over ½ cup slivered almonds, then broil and serve as above.

Pomegranate
Raita

Tomato, Cucumber, and # Onion Raita

Green Chutney

Cucumber and # Mint Raita

RAITAS
and
CHUTNEYS

Quick Tamarind Chutney

Pomegranate Raita

Serves 4

1 small pomegranate
1¾ cups plain yogurt
handful of chopped fresh cilantro
    leaves and stalks
salt and freshly ground black pepper,
    to taste
½ – ¾ teaspoon roasted cumin powder
    (seeds dry-roasted until red, then
    ground)
good pinch of red chili powder, to taste

This is a refreshing, tangy raita, vivid in both color and flavor, which brings a fresh sweetness to any Indian offering. These luscious fruits with jewel-like flesh come in different sizes, so use your judgment on how much fruit to add. There is no right answer, so add as much or as little as you like, testing the flavor as you go along.

Lightly press down on the pomegranate and roll with your hands on a hard surface, applying a little pressure so that you help to release the seeds on all sides. Slice in half and, working over a bowl, tap the outside of the fruit with a wooden spoon. The seeds should tumble out. There may be too many for the raita, so munch away.

Mix together the yogurt, most of the pomegranate seeds, and fresh cilantro. Season with salt, lots of black pepper, the cumin, and red chili powder. Garnish with a handful of pomegranate seeds and a few cilantro leaves.

Tomato, Cucumber, and Onion Raita

Serves 4

1 tomato, diced
1 small red onion, peeled and diced
5-in. piece of cucumber, peeled
    and diced
2 tablespoons fresh chopped cilantro
    leaves and stalks
1¾ cups plain yogurt
salt and freshly ground black pepper,
    to taste
½ – ¾ teaspoon roasted cumin powder
    (cumin seeds dry-roasted until red
    and ground)
¼ teaspoon red chili powder

This is one of the most common raitas, and the different textures and flavors make it a great accompaniment to any meal. Eat it as it is, or serve it as a cooling summer dip with crudités or naan wedges.

Mix together the vegetables, cilantro, and yogurt. Season with salt, plenty of black pepper, and the roasted cumin powder.

Tip into a serving bowl, sprinkle the chili powder over, and serve.

Cucumber and Mint Raita

Serves 4

5-in. piece of cucumber
3 tablespoons shredded fresh mint
1¾ cups plain yogurt
salt and freshly ground black pepper,
    to taste
¾ teaspoon roasted cumin powder
    (seeds dry-roasted until red, then
    ground)
good pinch of red chili powder

A great-tasting raita with the added bonus of having the combined cooling properties of mint, cucumber, yogurt, and cumin—a perfect way to counter heat in the food or in the air. Great with any meal or barbecue, or even just as a dip with naan or crudités.

Peel the cucumber, then coarsely grate and squeeze all the excess moisture from it.

Mix together the cucumber, mint, and yogurt. Stir in the seasoning and cumin powder. Sprinkle the red chili powder over to serve.

Opposite: *Pomegranate Raita, left; Cucumber and Mint Raita, top right; Tomato, Cucumber, and Onion Raita, bottom right.*

Raitas and Chutneys · 133

Serves 4–6

3 handfuls fresh mint leaves
1 small handful fresh cilantro leaves
½ clove of garlic, peeled
¼ small onion, peeled and chopped
1–2 green chilies, chopped (depending
    on how hot you like it)
12 raw pistachio nuts, shelled and
    chopped
¼ teaspoon dried mango powder or
    dried pomegranate powder
1 tablespoon lemon juice, or to taste
salt, to taste
2 tablespoons water

Green Chutney

This is an all-purpose chutney, known as hara chutni. It is eaten with North Indian snacks and broiled tandoori dishes, or even spread in sandwiches. Every home has its own recipe, which might be as simple as herbs, seasoning, and lemon juice. We often add dried mango powder, but if you don't have any, add more lemon juice. Pistachios help bind the chutney, which might otherwise become watery, but they can be omitted.

Simply purée all the ingredients for the chutney together in a food processor until smooth. Add as little water as possible, taste, and add more lemon juice if necessary—it should be herby and lemony. Store in clean screw-top jars in the fridge; it will keep for a few days.

Serves 6–8 with snacks

3 teaspoons thick tamarind paste
4 tablespoons brown or white sugar
½ teaspoon cumin seeds, dry roasted
    until fragrant and turning brown,
    then ground
¼ – ½ teaspoon freshly ground black
    pepper
¼ cup water

Quick Tamarind Chutney

In India the tamarind is used mainly to provide sourness to a dish and, in a curry, to help balance the sweetness from the onions that often form its base. Other than that, it is really popular in this sweet, tangy, and slightly spicy chutney. It is our version of ketchup and is served in even smaller quantities. Its natural partners are many of the northern tea-time snacks, such as vegetable samosas. The strength of the tamarind paste varies slightly from brand to brand. I have used a well-known brand I found in a local grocery store and noted that it contained salt, so I had no need to add any. Check the ingredients of your paste, and adjust the quantities of seasoning and sugar if necessary.

Put all the ingredients in a small saucepan, bring to a quick boil, then turn off the heat. Cool and serve judiciously.

This chutney can also be stored in screw-top jars in the fridge. It keeps well for weeks.

Nutty Saffron-flavored Yogurt

Steamed Yogurt

Strawberry Lassi

Mango Smoothie

The Ultimate Masala Tea

Coconut Candies

Lemon Lassi

Fennel Seed Drop Cookies

Coconut and Jaggery Pancakes

DRINKS
and
DESSERTS

Sandesh

Kulfi

Charantais Melon Rasayana

Orange-scented Rice Creams

Jaggery-caramelized Walnuts

Serves 4

4 cups whole-milk yogurt or
    2 cups Greek-style yogurt
2 teaspoons milk
½ – ¾ teaspoon saffron strands
6–8 tablespoons confectioners' sugar,
    or to taste (depends on the tartness
    of the yogurt)
¼ teaspoon freshly ground green
    cardamom powder, or to taste
3 tablespoons chopped unsalted
    pistachios
3 tablespoons slivered almonds,
    lightly roasted
pomegranate seeds, to garnish

Nutty Saffron-flavored Yogurt

This is a fantastic, vibrant dessert made with fresh yogurt. It is an amalgam of thick yogurt, summery, musky saffron, and aromatic green cardamom, with nuts for added texture. I like to scatter a handful of pomegranate seeds over the top for a burst of color and fruitiness. Yogurt will vary in its degree of tartness, depending on freshness, so add sugar according to taste. The potency of the saffron and cardamom powder also varies, depending on freshness and quality, so use my measurements as a guide.

Line a large strainer with a double layer of good-quality paper towels. Place over a bowl and pour in the yogurt. Refrigerate for as long as possible—at least 5–6 hours or until all the whey has drained off.

Heat the milk and crumble the saffron strands into the hot milk. Leave to infuse for 8–10 minutes, crushing the strands in the milk with the back of a spoon or your fingers.

Sift the sugar into the yogurt and stir in along with the saffron milk, cardamom powder, and half the nuts. Taste and adjust the sugar and cardamom powder, if necessary. Chill and serve garnished with the remaining nuts and pomegranate seeds.

Serves 4

2 cups set natural yogurt
generous ⅜ cup condensed milk
1½ tablespoon raisins (optional)
20 pistachios, roughly chopped,
    or 2 tablespoons slivered almonds,
      toasted
raspberries, to serve

Steamed Yogurt

It really surprises me how much you can do with yogurt and how every time I try something new, the results are always pleasantly surprising. The texture of this delicious dessert from Bengal is somewhere between a smooth panna cotta and a ricotta cheesecake. The longer you cook it, the grainier it becomes. This is not to say grainy is bad; some people prefer it one way, some the other. Raisins are optional—sometimes I like them in there, other times I just want some lovely seasonal fresh fruit. Soft fruits, such as raspberries, go really well with it.

Line a strainer with a double layer of paper towels, and place over a large bowl. Pour in the yogurt, and allow the whey to drain off for at least 5 hours. If you wish, you can leave it, covered, in the fridge overnight, but be sure to drain away any liquid in the bowl after the first 2 hours.

Preheat the oven to 350°F.

Whisk together the yogurt, condensed milk, and raisins (if using) until smooth. Divide the mixture between four small ramekins or ovenproof glasses. Cover each ramekin tightly with foil to prevent water from getting in. Place them in a baking dish, and pour in enough water to come a quarter of the way up the sides of the ramekins. Carefully place in the oven and cook for 30 minutes.

Cool the desserts in their dishes and chill overnight. Either serve in their dishes or turn out onto serving plates. Serve with the raspberries and sprinkle the nuts over the top.

Strawberry Lassi

Serves 2

1½ cups ripe strawberries
⅞ cup good-quality fresh plain yogurt
1½–2 tablespoons sugar, or to taste
ice cubes, to serve

One thing I love about the British summer is the strawberries—plump, sweet, and juicy. And whenever the sun starts shining and the temperature starts to rise, the Indian in me craves a lassi. This is the drink that is taken in the rural areas by the farmers to help cool down when working in their fields under a hot sun. It is traditionally made with buttermilk (the thin, slightly sour liquid that is the byproduct of making butter), but you can also use thinned-down plain yogurt.

Blend the strawberries, yogurt, and sugar together until frothy. Pour into glasses and serve with the ice.

Mango Smoothie

Serves 2

2 mangoes, preferably Alphonso
1¼ cups milk
2 tablespoons sugar, or to taste
lots of ice cubes, to serve

This drink is creamy and fruity; it is the pure essence of mango. The Indian mango season lasts all summer, and the king of the mango is the Alphonso—if you can find it, this is the one to buy. You can tell when it is ripe by its soft, yielding flesh and a sweet aroma. I have given approximate quantities, as mangoes differ in size and sweetness, so add and taste as you go along until you are happy. Chill the smoothies well before serving.

Standing the mango upright with the narrow end toward you, slice off both cheeks on either side of the stone. Slice these in half lengthwise, and remove the skin by peeling or slicing. Slice off the remaining sides of the stone as much as possible. Repeat with the second mango, and put all the flesh and juices in a blender.

Add the milk and sugar, and blend to a thick, smooth mass. Pour into glasses, each filled with ice cubes, and serve chilled.

Lemon Lassi

Serves 2

1 cup good-quality fresh plain yogurt
⅞ cup water
3 tablespoons sugar, or to taste
2–3 teaspoons lemon juice, or to taste
finely grated zest of 1½ small lemons
ice cubes, to serve
2 sprigs of fresh mint

This lassi is really refreshing, and the fragrance of the lemon zest is pure summer. Good-quality, fresh yogurt will stop this drink from being too tart. I love it—it is better than lemonade and lighter than a milkshake or smoothie. Perfect for a healthy, outdoor life.

Blend together the yogurt, water, sugar, lemon juice, and zest until light and frothy. Adjust the sugar and lemon to taste. Pour into tall glasses filled with ice cubes and the mint, and serve.

Opposite: *Mango Smoothie, left; Strawberry Lassi, right.*

Serves 4

4 cups whole milk
2 tablespoons ground almonds
1 tablespoon rice flour
5–6 tablespoons sugar, or to taste
⅓ – ½ teaspoon green cardamom
    powder, or to taste
2 tablespoons chopped pistachios
2 tablespoons slivered almonds

Kulfi

Kulfi is a traditional Indian ice cream but made without cream and without eggs. At its simplest, it is a blend of reduced milk and sugar, flavored with green cardamom powder. Restaurants normally add cream to the mixture. I have enriched my basic recipe by adding in some ground almonds and rice flour, but you can make a simpler version by doubling the quantity of milk and leaving out the almonds and flour. It takes a long time to make and does require some loving attention, but if you tend to hover around the kitchen, it's really easy to make. Just remember that you need to stir the mixture frequently to prevent the milk from catching on the base of the saucepan and burning.

Heat the milk in a wide, heavy-based pan over a low heat and bring to a boil. Then lower the heat and cook gently, stirring often. Place the ground almonds and flour in a small cup, and once the milk is warm, stir in a little milk, make a thin paste, and stir back into the pan with the sugar. Continue to cook gently, as the milk needs to reduce by half—this takes about an hour. If a skin forms on the surface, just stir it back in.

Stir in the cardamom powder to taste. Cool completely, then decant into four kulfi molds (I also know of it being set in Styrofoam cups or normal freezerproof containers). If you have the time, 2 hours after it has been put into the freezer, take it out and give it a good whisk to break up any ice crystals.

I recommend keeping the ice cream in the freezer for about 5–6 hours. Take the molds out of the freezer 20 minutes before serving. Dip them briefly in hot water to loosen, then turn out onto serving plates. Sprinkle generously with the nuts.

**Makes 12 small pancakes
or 8 larger ones**

Pancakes

scant ⅜ cup all-purpose flour
pinch of salt
1 tablespoon sugar
1 egg
⅝ cup milk
scant 2 tablespoons unsalted butter,
    melted, plus extra for frying

Filling

3 oz. jaggery, broken into small pieces,
    or scant ½ cup muscovado or good-
    quality dark brown sugar
⅞ cup fresh grated coconut
¾ cup roasted salted cashew nuts,
    broken up

Coconut and Jaggery Pancakes

These filled pancakes are a lovely dessert, but can also be served as breakfast for the kids. I make fine, French-style crêpes, as they are delicate and light and are perfect for desserts, rather than heavier American-style pancakes, which would require more filling. I add salted cashews to this sweet filling because I think the salt just brings out the sweetness of the sugar and coconut, but you can add plain roasted cashews or leave them out altogether. These pancakes freeze really well (separate them with waxed paper and wrap well). I have a small 5-in. pancake pan, which is the perfect dessert size, but use whatever size of pan you have and just be aware of quantities.

Sift the flour into a large bowl, and add the salt and sugar. Make a well in the middle and crack in the egg, then pour in the melted butter. Using a whisk, slowly bring the sides of the flour into the well and mix until you have a smooth paste. Whisk in the milk and leave to rest for 30 minutes.

Meanwhile, mix together the ingredients for the filling.

Heat the pan until hot. Add a little butter and, when melted, pour in a ladleful or half a ladleful of batter, depending on the size of your pan. You want a thin covering. Turn the heat to medium, and after 30 seconds or so, using a flat metal spatula, flip the pancake over. Cook the other side for another 15–20 seconds or until the underside has a few brown spots.

Continue cooking the pancakes this way but without adding any more butter to the pan. Stack the pancakes on a plate, separating them with waxed paper.

When you are ready to eat, place 1–1½ heaped tablespoons of filling on one half of the pancake and fold. You can heat the filling in the pan if you wish, which will melt the sugar, and you can heat the pancakes in the oven at the same time. This dessert is great served with a scoop of vanilla ice cream.

Makes 12

4 cups whole milk
scant ¹/₄–⁵/₈ cup yogurt (depends how
    sour the yogurt is), beaten
generous ¹/₈ cup fine granulated sugar
good pinch of saffron, powdered in a
    pestle and mortar with ¹/₄ teaspoon
    sugar
¹/₂ teaspoon green cardamom powder
    (seeds taken out of the pods and
    ground)

Other flavoring ideas

1 tablespoon rose water, or to taste
³/₄ teaspoon vanilla extract, or to taste
¹/₃ cup shelled pistachio nuts, pounded
    to a rough purée (add an extra
    tablespoon sugar to the cheese and
    add 1 tablespoon milk)
good-quality chocolate powder, to taste
3 tablespoons shredded coconut, or
    to taste

To garnish

chopped pistachios, slivered almonds,
    saffron strands, coconut flakes, or
    rose petals

Sandesh

To say that these little sweetmeats are made of fresh white cheese and sugar will not convey just how delicious they are. They are really tempting, and when you learn there is no added fat, you feel able to give in. These Bengali sweets are one of the most popular in a region renowned for its sweets, and they are one of the few still made at home in a culture that outsourced sweet-making a long time ago.

Bring the milk to a boil in a pan set over a low heat. Once the milk starts to rise in the pan, stir in the yogurt. The milk will curdle, leaving curdlike cheese floating in murky water. If it does not split, add some more yogurt and leave for 20 seconds over the heat.

Line a strainer with muslin or cheesecloth and place over a large bowl or saucepan. Strain the cheese into the lined strainer and discard the water. Run fresh tap water over the cheese to remove any sourness from the yogurt. Twist the cloth around the cheese to make a tight ball, and place it under a weight (I fill the pan with water and place it on top). Leave to drain for 20 minutes.

Place the cheese in a blender with the sugar, and pulse three times to make a slightly grainy paste. Spoon the mixture into a cold nonstick skillet and place over a low–moderate heat, stirring continuously for about 3–5 minutes. The mixture should leave the base of the pan and have the texture of soft dough. It will dry more as it cools. If in doubt, take a small bit and roll it into a small ball. It shouldn't crack and should hold its shape without being hard.

Now the basic mixture is ready. Add the saffron and the cardamom powder and roll into small walnut-sized balls. Garnish with chopped pistachios, slivered almonds, saffron strands, coconut flakes, or rose petals, depending on the flavoring. Chill until ready to eat.

Serves 4

4½ tablespoons rice flour
2 tablespoons ground almonds
4 cups whole milk
4 tablespoons sugar
½–¾ teaspoon green cardamom powder
1 heaped teaspoon grated orange zest,
    or to taste
10 pistachios, blanched, peeled, and
    sliced
10 almonds, blanched, skinned, and
    sliced, or slivered almonds
slices of blood orange, to garnish

Orange-scented Rice Creams

This is a popular, classic North Indian dessert, known as phirni. I have enlivened the recipe by adding orange zest, which goes wonderfully with the warming cardamom. The rice flour helps the milk to set into an dreamy, aromatic mass, with the ground almonds providing just enough bite. The creams are made a day in advance of serving so they have a chance to set and chill. Freshly ground cardamom has more flavor than store-bought varieties, so taste and adjust, if necessary. I set the creams in individual bowls or sometimes cocktail glasses, for a little glamour, but you can use one large bowl and serve straight from there. For a richer version, replace some of the milk with heavy cream.

Mix the rice flour and ground almonds in ⅝ cup of the milk to make a smooth paste. Heat the remaining milk in a pan on a medium heat, stirring constantly. As you bring it up to a simmer, stir in the rice flour mixture.

Cook, stirring, over a medium heat for 10 minutes. Add the sugar, cardamom, and orange zest, and continue cooking for about 3–4 minutes until it reaches a semithick custard consistency. Pour into your serving dish of choice and chill. Garnish with the nuts and slices of orange before serving.

1½ cups Charantais melon flesh, cut
     into small dice
1 cup fresh or canned coconut milk
2 tablespoons sugar, or to taste
     (depending on sweetness of melon)
seeds from ½ a pomegranate
2 handfuls of crushed ice
handful of slivered almonds, lightly
     roasted in the oven until just
     changing color

Charantais Melon Rasayana

This wonderful seasonal fruit is the striped melon with the orange flesh. If you cannot find it, use cantaloupe or muskmelon instead. Check that it is ripe by sniffing one end—it should give off a fruity aroma. The Charantais melon is juicy and sweet and perfect in this refreshing South Indian-inspired dessert. The melon leaks into the creamy coconut and is enlivened by the pomegranate seeds.

Place the melon dice in a deep bowl. Using your fingers, crush them slightly so that they are no longer regular in shape and start to leak out their wonderful juice, but do not let them become mushy. Add the coconut milk and sugar and mix well. The color should be a beautiful pale peach; you may want to give the melon another crush to assimilate the other ingredients. Stir in the pomegranate and chill until ready to serve.

Place a tablespoon of crushed ice in the bottom of the serving bowls and top with the fruit mixture. Sprinkle the slivered almonds over and serve cold.

Serves 3 to munch on or 5 as a garnish

3½ oz. jaggery sugar, chopped or
    pounded into smallish pieces, or
    generous ½ cup muscovado or
    good-quality dark brown sugar
¾ cup walnut halves

Jaggery-caramelized Walnuts

I love these little bites, which can also be used as a garnish for creamy Indian puddings or as a topping for plain yogurt. They take just minutes to make. We already know that walnuts are good for us, but jaggery is amazing. It is a flavorful, completely unrefined sugar sold in blocks and renowned for its health properties. It is full of iron and other minerals and is known to help keep your lungs clean—in fact, many factories in Delhi give their workers a nugget every day to keep them healthy while working in a dusty environment. The best jaggery is quite dark and hard and needs to be chopped and pestle-and-mortared. It can be found in Indian stores, and although some supermarkets have started to stock it, theirs is a softer, more watery version of the real thing. Either will work, but the darker jaggery has a more molasses-like flavor.

Place the jaggery in a saucepan and stir over a low–moderate heat to melt. Stir frequently to help it melt faster. When smooth, stir in the walnut halves. Stir to coat properly, and cook for 1–2 minutes or until the jaggery has darkened in color.

Place the walnuts individually on a sheet of baking paper or turn out onto an oiled plate. If using jaggery, you have to work quickly, as the jaggery will start to harden. If so, heat the pan a little to melt it again.

Store in an airtight container when cool.

The Ultimate Masala Tea

Makes 1 large cupful

1½ cups water
scant ½ cup milk
4 black peppercorns
10 green cardamom pods
good pinch of green fennel seeds
small stick of cinnamon
1 in. fresh ginger (see page 12), roughly
    sliced
1 tea bag (I use a common black tea
    blend)
sugar, to taste
slightest pinch of salt (optional)

This is the ultimate cup of tea.
It is what women across India
make when they have friends
over. It offers solace and
comfort and is invigorating and
relaxing all at the same time.
I drink a cup every morning
without fail, and no other tea
does it for me anymore.

Heat the water, milk, spices, and
ginger in a pan. Once it comes to a
boil, reduce the heat and cook over
a low–moderate heat for 15 minutes.
Be careful, as the milk easily boils
over. If this is about to happen,
reduce the heat and take the pan
off the heat for a few seconds.

Once reduced to a large cupful,
add the tea bag, and let it brew for
1 minute, or more if you like strong
tea. Strain into your cup and add
sugar or salt to taste.

Opposite: *Masala Tea with Fennel
Seed Drop Cookies*

Fennel Seed Drop Cookies

Makes 20

⅝ cup all purpose flour
⅓ cup fine granulated sugar
2 slightly rounded tablespoons skim
    milk powder
⅝ cup milk
1 black cardamom pod (optional), seeds
    removed and pounded in a mortar
    and pestle
1½ teaspoons fennel seeds, ground
pinch of salt
1 tablespoon ground almonds
2 tablespoons melted butter
4 tablespoons ghee or vegetable oil,
    for frying

These simple cookies resemble
little pancakes. They are
normally deep-fried, soaked in
sugar syrup, and served with
thick, sweet, milky desserts. I
have added sugar to the batter
and pan-fried them, keeping all
the flavors but simplifying the
cooking and lightening the dish.

Mix together the flour, sugar,
powdered and whole milk, spices,
salt, almonds, and butter into a
batter. Leave to rest for 10 minutes.

Heat the oil or ghee in a nonstick
skillet and drop small tablespoons
of batter into the pan, keeping
them separate. Fry over a moderate
heat for about 1 minute on each
side, until golden on both sides.
Drain the cookies on a plate lined
with paper towels. They are best
served while still warm, crisp on
the edges and chewy on the inside.

Coconut Candies

Makes 18–20

generous ¾ cup grated fresh coconut,
    or shredded, if necessary
1 cup whole milk
scant ½ cup sugar
¼ teaspoon green cardamom seeds,
    ground
1 tablespoon unsalted butter
2 tablespoons chopped pistachios

These sweet bites are easy
to make. The only tricky bit is
removing the coconut flesh, but
you can substitute shredded.
Either buy a coconut scraper
(see page 10), or break the
coconut and carefully remove
the flesh by getting a small
paring knife under the brown
skin and levering it out.

Place the coconut, milk, and sugar
in a nonstick pan, and cook over a
low heat for 20 minutes, stirring
often. By now the mixture should
come together in a lump. It you
take a little bit in your fingers, it
should be easy to roll and will set.
If it is still too moist, cook for a
couple more minutes and try again.

Add the cardamom and butter. Cook,
stirring, for another 3 minutes. The
coconut will color slightly and come
together really easily.

Make into little balls by rolling
between your palms. Place on a
plate and sprinkle the chopped
pistachios over. If you can resist
them, the candies will keep well
in the fridge, stored in an airtight
container.

Glossary

Besides the more familiar English translations for ingredients, I've also given the Indian names, which you may come across in Indian stores.

Spices

Asafetida (heeng)
A really pungent powder that helps digestion and as such is added to many dishes that are hard to digest. Use the smallest pinch, as it is very strong. If you don't have any, leave it out—it won't affect the dish too much.

Black/brown cardamom pod (badi elaichi)
These large woody pods look as though they are well past their sell-by date, but have a wonderful and strong flavor when cooked. They are an important element in garam masala and pilaffs.

Black peppercorns (kali mirch)
Little needs to be said here, except that the taste and aroma of freshly ground peppercorns is far superior to store-bought powder.

Brown mustard seeds (rai)
These brown seeds are used a lot in India. It is to the south what cumin is to the north. It is also a key element in making relishes. When added to hot oil, the seeds will splutter, so it is good to have a cover handy to stop them from popping out of the pan. Once cooked, they become almost nutty. When ground into a powder, they give a tart note to dishes, and when ground into a paste, they are the very essence of mustard.

Carom seeds (ajwain)
A small, dark green seed that is reminiscent of thyme. It is quite strong, so you need to use only a little. We often use it with fish and in some Indian breads. It is also an instantaneous cure for a stomach ache. Take half a teaspoonful with a pinch of salt and drink with hot water.

Chaat masala
A blend of spices that few Indians make at home (if you have trouble finding it, you can find simple recipes for it on the Internet). It is spicy and tart, and Indians sprinkle it over many cooked foods or even drinks for a kick of flavor.

Cinnamon/cassia bark (dal chini)
Cassia bark is used more than cinnamon in India and has a smoother flavor. Use either sparingly, as both have a big flavor and can overpower others. I add it in small sticks—any more and it will be too much.

Cloves (laung)
A strong spice, which is most commonly used in garam masala. The natural oil in this is great for a toothache—bite down on the clove where it hurts, and hold it there for as long as possible.

Coriander seeds and powder (sabut dhaniya)
Coriander seeds come from the flowers of the coriander, or cilantro, plant. They are wonderfully mild and aromatic and are abundantly used. They have a subtle flavor, but once you know what they taste like, you can always identify their presence. I often drink a coriander-seed tea after meals, as it helps digestion and is cooling on the body. The powdered seeds are used as a base for many masalas, and it is probably the most used spice in my kitchen. Good-quality store-bought powder will be mossy green rather than brown.

Cumin seeds (jira)
This familiar spice is earthy when cooked in oil and nutty when dry-roasted. It is an important spice in our cooking and adds a lovely rounded flavor. Great for digestion when made into a light, warm tea.

Dried mango powder (amchur)
This ingredient is actually made from dried raw mangoes. It is tangy, and we often sprinkle it on cooked tandoori foods or fried potatoes, instead of lemon juice or vinegar. It doesn't need cooking.

Fennel seeds/aniseeds (saunf)
A sweet, licorice-like spice. The seeds are often seen in the cuisine of Kashmir but also in the south. They are good for the stomach, and cooling and great for breast-feeding when infused in hot water. Also a natural breath freshener—chew on a few after a meal.

Fenugreek seeds (methr)
Strong, bitter seeds, which have that familiar "curry" flavor. Use very little at any time.

Garam masala
This famous blend is at its purest composed of the strong flavors of cloves, black cardamom, cinnamon, and green cardamom. We add bay leaves, mace, and black peppercorn to this. Many milder brands will add coriander and cumin seeds. This powder can be added toward the end of cooking for a real punch of aroma or closer to the beginning for a more rounded, subtle taste.

Green cardamom pod (chotti elaichi)
This is one of my favorite spices. It has a soft but powerful aroma and is used in sweet and savory dishes and is essential in spicy tea. The seeds can be ground to make green cardamom powder.

Mace (javitri)
A wonderful flavor, which goes very well with meat and chicken.

Nigella seeds (kalonji)
These delicate black seeds have a peppery flavor but without the bite.

Red chili powder (lal mirch)
This is usually very hot and adds great color to a dish but not much flavor.

Saffron (kesa)
Saffron is the dried stamen of the crocus flower. It is very expensive, but a little goes a long way, and it keeps well in the fridge. A lovely, musky flavor that works in both savory and sweet dishes. Try to find long stamens.

Turmeric powder (haldi)
This vibrant powder is essential in Indian cooking. It is prized for its color and its fantastic medicinal properties.

White poppy seeds (khus khus)
These are the same as the familiar dark poppy seeds but without the black husk and have a smoother character.

Lentils

Bengal gram (channa dal)
The whole bean is similar to the chickpea but is smaller and with a dark brown skin. Once skinned and split, the bean becomes a wonderful, earthy, yellow lentil.

Split and skinned black gram (urad dal)
This small, delicate lentil (also called Beluga lentils) is used a lot in South Indian food for texture, as it is sautéed to a nutty crunch without being pre-boiled.

Split and skinned mung bean (dhuli mung ki dal)
This small, pale yellow lentil is one of the easiest to digest and has a subtle, buttery flavor. At home, this is the lentil we eat most.

Split yellow pigeon pea lentil (toovar/arhar dal)
This lentil is often cooked until it completely breaks down to a smooth paste and is then spiced before being served. Wash well, as it is usually coated in a film of oil to help preserve it.

Flours

Chapati flour
A blend of wholewheat and white, all-purpose flour, which is used to make our most common flatbreads. It can be found in Indian stores as well as some larger supermarkets. Substitute with equal quantities of all-purpose and wholewheat flour.

Chickpea (gram) flour (besan)
A key ingredient in Indian cookery and made from powdered Bengal gram. The North Indians use it to make batters, to bind marinades in tandoori foods, to flavor vegetables, and also to make simple wheat-free breads. It has more protein than wheat. It can now be found in some large supermarkets.

Rice flour
In India rice flour would be made by soaking the grains, drying them in the sun, and then grinding them to a fine powder. This is used to add crispness to fried foods, to make dumplings (in the south), to thicken curries and (in the north) to make a ground rice pudding. A delicate and fragrant flour, which I love and use as a thickener instead of cornstarch.

Others

Buttermilk
A byproduct of the butter-making process. It may seem like a tangy version of skim milk, but, once flavored, it is absolutely delicious and easier to digest than ordinary milk or yogurt.

Curry leaves (kari patta)
These leaves are truly fragrant. They add a taste of the south to a dish. If you have trouble finding these leaves, you might grow your own. *Helichrysum italicum* ssp. *serotinum* is hardy in zones 8–10.

Ghee (clarified butter)
Prized for its medicinal qualities in the East. It has a strong aroma and burns at a higher temperature than butter. See also page 12.

Jaggery (gur)
This is a completely unrefined sugar and probably the most healthful sugar around. It is made by boiling the natural sap from the date palm until it is hard and sets in a block. It is full of minerals and has a host of healthy properties. Workers in dusty Delhi factories are given little nuggets of jaggery to help keep their lungs clean. If you cannot find jaggery, muscovado or good-quality dark brown sugar can be substituted.

Paneer
This traditional Indian cheese is made without rennet or bacterial culture (see page 26). It is similar to fresh farmer's cheese and looks like solid ricotta. I think it is fabulous. Paneer is an important source of protein for Indian vegetarians.

Pilaff
A term used for any spiced and seasoned rice dish. It can be simple or contain any number of added ingredients.

Raita
A term used for yogurt once it has had ingredients added to it. You can add cooked or raw, crunchy vegetables or even fruit to it. A wonderful summery dish that is great with any barbecues as well as complete Indian meals.

Tamarind (imli)
The tamarind tree bears wonderful pods of fruit, which are thick, fibrous, and full of large seeds. But once softened and strained, the tamarind paste is a wonderful, tangy ingredient. It has a fruity, sour flavor and is used prolifically in the south, often to balance the sweetness of the coconut in their curries. The ready-made paste is available from some supermarkets, but brands differ in strength, so add according to taste.

Tandoori cooking
A tandoor is a barrel-shaped clay oven. Food cooked in this way is so popular that it is now eaten all over the world. The temperature in a tandoor can reach 500°F and gives dishes a barbecue-like flavor by searing it on the outside.

Index

Suppliers

If you live in a town or city with a reasonably large Indian population, you should be able to find a grocery store that stocks the ingredients required for these recipes. And many of the ingredients can be found in a good-sized supermarket. Alternatively, try the Internet. Some useful Web sites:

www.indianfoodsco.com • www.ishopindian.com • www.penzeys.com • www.wholefoodsmarket.com

Acknowledgments

Writing a book is always a production. Like an Indian wedding, it involves many key people without whom it wouldn't have been possible. I want to thank my husband for always believing in me and everything I do. Thanks also to my sister, for always being so supportive and so generous with her time, filling in any gaps of loneliness in my daughter's life. To Heather, for being such a fantastic agent and ambassador. To Elly, for being so helpful and calm during the many periods of madness. To the powers-that-be in the BBC for giving me this fantastic opportunity and for such a wonderful experience. And last, but by no means least, to the team at Quadrille for succeeding so effortlessly in putting together this beautiful book in record time.